The Power of Somatic Therapy

Unlock Your Inner Strength with Simple Tools and Exercises to Manage Stress and Trauma, Cultivate Self-Compassion, and Build Resilience by Awakening the Mind-Body Connection

K. D. ANNE

Contents

Introduction

There was a moment in my life that was so raw and eye-opening that it felt like the universe had sat me down for a heart-to-heart. I was navigating through a particularly stormy season of stress and unresolved feelings, feeling more disconnected from my body with each passing day. It was during this time that I stumbled upon somatic therapy. This wasn't just another self-help trend but a lifeline, pulling me gently toward a place of profound healing and understanding. I remember the first session vividly—the sensation of genuinely inhabiting my body for the first time in years, the flood of relief and realization. It was a turning point that set me on the path I walk today.

So, what exactly is somatic therapy? Imagine that your body is a storeroom of every experience, emotion, and memory you've ever had. Somatic therapy is the key that unlocks that storeroom, allowing you to explore, understand, and integrate these aspects of yourself through the body, not just the mind. It's about creating a dialogue between your physical and emotional selves, using simple yet profound techniques to foster healing and resilience.

This book aims to extend that key to you. Whether you're battling stress, seeking to overcome trauma, or simply wishing to cultivate a deeper connection with yourself, this guide is designed to empower you with the tools and exercises of somatic therapy. It's more than just a book; it's a companion on your journey toward unlocking your inner strength and resilience.

What sets this book apart is its wealth of information and the transformation it invites. Through a combination of personal stories, practical exercises, and a step-by-step approach, I aim to make somatic therapy not just accessible but deeply personal and immediately applicable. This book is crafted to be actively used, to live on your coffee table, dog-eared and underlined, a testament to your journey of growth and healing.

Somatic therapy is a universal language, speaking to the heart of what it means to be human. It's not reserved for those in recovery; it's a powerful tool for anyone looking to manage everyday stress, deepen their mindfulness practice, or feel more alive in their skin. Its benefits are as broad and varied as the individuals it serves.

The book is divided into three main parts in the following pages: Foundations of Somatic Therapy, Techniques and Exercises, and Integrating Somatic Therapy into Your Life. This structure is designed to guide you gently but confidently through the principles, practices, and, ultimately, the incorporation of somatic therapy into your daily existence. The book offers many examples of working with a therapist, and you can also work on your own. The choice is yours.

I invite you to embark on this journey of self-discovery and healing with an open mind and heart. Create a sacred space for yourself to engage with these practices, reflect on your experiences, and observe your evolution. This book is a starting point, a gateway to a deeper understanding of yourself and your capacity for resilience and joy.

As we begin this journey together, know that I am here, cheering you on every step of the way. Believe in yourself and the transformative power of somatic therapy, for I truly believe in you. Let's awaken the mind-body connection and unlock the door to a more integrated, vibrant life.

Chapter 1

Integrating Body and Mind

Exploring the Foundations and Efficacies of Somatic Therapy

"Trauma is a fact of life, but it doesn't have to be a life sentence."
– Peter Levine

Congratulations on making the decision to prioritize yourself! Our busy lives often make us believe we don't have enough time to care for our well-being. However, if we don't make time today to be mindful of our thoughts, breath, and body, we may have to deal with unwanted health issues in the future. The beauty of somatic therapy is that you have the choice to dedicate minutes or hours a day to your personalized routine. Remember, you deserve to take time for yourself!

I encourage you to keep a journal close by. It doesn't have to be fancy. You can simply use a notebook and dedicate it entirely to this book and your incredible journey, which begins now.

How to Maximize Your Experience with This Book

The definition of keywords has been marked with a star to facilitate understanding for those who may be new to the concept.

★ Definition of Keywords

Tools and techniques are indicated in bold as bullet points. You will notice them throughout each chapter.

- **Tools and techniques**

You will find a summary of all the tools and techniques at the end of each chapter.

The best way to start with this practice is to read through each chapter and follow the guidelines for each tool and technique. Some will resonate with you, and some won't. Everyone has unique needs, which can fluctuate over time. Trust your instincts. Know what you are feeling and what is right for you. There is no right or wrong way of working toward your goals.

Chapters 1 through 7 will help you discover what works for you, and Chapter 8 will guide you in personalizing your daily practice.

I have included a BONUS chapter on **Empowering the Self** featuring somatics to strengthen relationships, overcome limiting beliefs, practice mindful eating, and so much more!

Welcome to *The Power of Somatic Therapy*!

Let's Start with a Very Simple 3-Minute Exercise

- Close your eyes and plant your feet flat on the ground while sitting up straight.

- Take five slow, deep breaths, and notice where your breath is coming from. It might be from the chest or maybe from the belly. It might feel restricted where you feel like you can't go very deep. Notice if it gets deeper with each breath.

- After your last deep breath, just sit with the sensations in your body for about 30 seconds.

Open your eyes and write down any sensations you notice within your body.

Now, I invite you to take a moment to think about what you would like to work on during this journey and **check each one** that applies to you. Once you have read this entire book, you will see how far you've come.

I want to:

- manage stress

- manage anxiety

- manage panic attacks

- overcome depression

- recover from trauma

- manage chronic pain

- improve sleep

- become more joyful

- strengthen my relationships

- overcome limiting beliefs

- practice mindful eating

- understand what my body is telling me

- work on my personal growth

Embodiment

The Essential Principle of Somatic Therapy

★ Embodiment

Embodiment is living in a way that fully embraces and expresses one's physical and emotional experiences.

In the heart of a bustling city, under the glow of the neon lights, there lies a quiet room. Within its walls, individuals from all walks of life gather, each carrying their own unique burdens, hopes, and fears. This setting, though simple, is the stage for a profound transformation. The silent dialogue between mind and body unfolds in this space through somatic therapy. Here, in the tangible quiet and the shared breaths of strangers, we begin to understand the profound importance of embodiment—the core principle that sustains the intricate dance of somatic therapy.

Embodiment is not just a concept or a fleeting state of awareness; it is the experience of being fully present within our bodies and feeling the weight of our existence in every cell and breath. It's the foundation upon which somatic therapy constructs its healing practices, aiming to bridge the gaps that trauma, stress, and disconnection have created between our physical selves and our emotional lives.

Understanding Embodiment

To grasp the essence of embodiment, one must first recognize the body as more than a vessel or a bystander to our mental and emotional experiences. It is an active participant, a repository of memory, emotion, and intuition. The body speaks in the language of sensations—a tightening in the chest, a flutter in the stomach, the weight of exhaustion on our shoulders. These sensations are the body's way of communicating, telling us stories about our needs, fears, and desires. Embodiment is tuning into this language, learning to listen and respond to the body's signals with curiosity and compassion.

Clinical Applications

In therapy, particularly within the somatic approach, embodiment takes center stage. Therapists guide their clients in exploring and interpreting the physical sensations accompanying emotional states, using techniques that foster a deeper connection to the body. This might involve movement, breathwork, or mindfulness practices, encouraging clients to observe and interact with their physical experiences in real-time. With its promise of confidentiality and understanding, the therapist's office becomes a lab for this exploration. In this place, clients can safely experiment with connecting to their bodies without judgment.

For example, a therapist might notice a client's clenched fists as they discuss a stressful event. By gently bringing attention to this physical manifestation of stress, the therapist invites the client to explore the sensation, breathe into it, and perhaps understand its source. This process not only aids in emotional regulation but also empowers the client, offering them tangible tools to cope with stress and anxiety outside the therapy session.

Experiential Learning

The beauty of embodiment lies in its inherently experiential nature. It cannot be fully comprehended through reading or discussion alone; it must be lived, felt, and practiced. This is why somatic therapy heavily emphasizes experiential learning, inviting clients to engage directly with their physical sensations and observe various exercises' effects on their emotional state. Through this hands-on approach, clients develop a more nuanced understanding of their bodies as they learn to navigate their internal landscapes with greater ease and awareness.

Consider the act of grounding, for example. A therapist might guide a client through a grounding exercise, asking them to focus on the sensation of their feet against the floor and notice the stability of the earth beneath them. As the client directs their attention to these physical sensations, they may find their racing thoughts beginning to slow and their breath deepening. This experience, simple yet profound, offers a concrete example of how the body can be a resource for emotional regulation and stress relief.

Therapeutic Outcomes

The journey toward increased embodiment is transformative, with far-reaching mental and emotional well-being implications. Clients in somatic therapy often report an enhanced sense of self-awareness and a deeper connection to their emotional lives. This newfound intimacy with the self fosters resilience.

★Resilience

Resilience is the ability to recover quickly from difficulties—emotional strength.

Resilience enables individuals to navigate challenges with greater flexibility and grace. By learning to listen to and honor their bodies' signals, clients develop a more compassionate relationship with themselves, laying the groundwork for lasting healing and growth.

Embodiment is a therapeutic tool and a way of being, a lens through which we can experience the world more fully.

Decoding the Language of Your Body

Our bodies speak volumes, whispering secrets of our inner worlds through a language as old as time. This dialect of discomfort, joy, tension, and relaxation is the body's way of communicating, often unnoticed yet profoundly impactful. To decode this language is to hold a mirror to our souls, reflecting the truths beneath the surface of our conscious minds.

Body Signals

The dialogue begins with the subtle signals our bodies send us, a lexicon of sensations that guide us through the landscapes of our emotions. A clenched jaw might speak of suppressed anger, while a sudden flutter in the stomach may signal anticipation or fear. Though seemingly mundane, these signals are the body's attempt to communicate its needs and reactions—a somatic Morse code that, when deciphered, can offer deep insights into our emotional states.

Consider the act of breathing, a function so automatic that it fades into the backdrop of our lives. Yet, in moments of stress, our breath quickens, shallow and sharp, as if echoing the pace of our racing thoughts. By tuning into this change, acknowledging it, and consciously slowing our breathing, we initiate a dialogue with our bodies that can soothe the disruption of our minds and bring us back to a state of harmony.

Emotional Connections

The connection between physical sensations and emotions is not coincidental. Our nervous system, a vast network of signals and responses, does not differentiate between physical and emotional pain; distress is distress, regardless of its origin. This intertwining of the physical and emotional realms suggests that by listening to our bodies, we can gain insight into our emotional landscape, navigating its peaks and valleys with a newfound map.

Imagine standing before a crowd, the spotlight casting a warm glow on your skin. The familiar flutter of nerves dances in your stomach, and your palms are damp with anticipation. At this moment, your body is a compass, pointing toward the underlying emotion—perhaps excitement, perhaps fear. By acknowledging these sensations, you allow yourself to fully inhabit the moment and embrace the fear, transforming it into a source of strength and vitality.

Shared Experiences

The transformative power of decoding the body's language has been confirmed in countless therapeutic encounters.

For years, my friend Monica carried the weight of unresolved grief on her shoulders—a burden so familiar she had stopped noticing it. It was only through somatic therapy that she was finally able to confront the physical manifestation of her pain. Through this process, she started to untangle the complex feelings of grief and was eventually able to let go of them. Even though it was an emotional journey, she realized that her physical state played a crucial role in her healing, proving the undeniable connection between the mind and body.

One of my colleagues, John, suffered from anxiety, his days overshadowed by a lingering sense of unease that seemed to have no source. Through somatic therapy, he learned to recognize the tightness in his chest as a signal of his anxiety, a physical manifestation of his fears. By focusing on this sensation, breathing into it, and gradually learning to relax his muscles, he unraveled the knot of his anxiety, gaining a sense of control and peace that had eluded him for years.

Practical Exercises

The journey toward understanding the body's language is one of practice and patience, a gradual tuning into the whispers of our physical selves. A simple yet powerful exercise in this endeavor is the practice of body scanning.

★Body Scanning

Body scanning is a mindful exploration of bodily sensations traversing the body from head to toe.

This practice fosters a deeper connection to your body and offers a moment of stillness in the rush of daily life—a pause in which to listen and learn.

- **Body Scanning**: Lie still, close your eyes, and direct your attention to each part of your body. Notice the sensations that dwell within—tension, warmth, discomfort, or ease.

Another exercise involves journaling in response to physical sensations.

★Journaling

Journaling is a reflective practice that bridges the gap between body and mind.

- **Journaling:** Write down your thoughts and feelings when a particular sensation arises—a headache, a flutter of nerves, or a sense of relaxation. Explore the possible emotional connections.

Over time, this practice can reveal patterns, shed light on how your body responds to various emotional states, and offer clues to navigate your inner world more effectively.

The Neurobiology of Trauma and Healing

In the labyrinth of the human mind, where emotions and memories intertwine, the impact of trauma stands as a stark disruptor, altering the very fabric of our neurological and bodily functions. This dissonance affects the psyche and imprints itself upon the body, manifesting in many physical symptoms that echo the emotional turmoil. Through the lens of somatic therapy, an exploration into the neurobiology of trauma and healing reveals the intricate dialogue between the brain and the body. This conversation holds the key to transformative healing.

★Mind-Body Connection

Mind-body connection is the belief that physical health and emotional well-being are closely linked.

Trauma, in its many forms, acts as a shockwave through the system, affecting areas of the brain responsible for processing threat and safety, such as the amygdala, hippocampus, and prefrontal cortex. This neural upheaval disrupts the brain's ability to regulate emotions and bodily responses, leading to a state of hyperarousal or numbing, symptoms often associated with post-traumatic stress disorder (PTSD). At the same time, the body responds to these neural distress signals by adopting patterns of tension, altered breathing, and other somatic markers of stress, creating a feedback loop that perpetuates the trauma response.

In healing, the interconnectivity of the brain and body serves as a foundation for somatic therapy. By focusing on bodily sensations and fostering a mindful awareness of physical experiences, somatic therapy seeks to interrupt this feedback loop, offering new pathways for the brain to process and integrate traumatic memories. This approach not only addresses the psychological aspects of trauma but also acknowledges and works with its physical manifestations, embodying a holistic path to recovery.

★Healing Processes

The healing journey is the personal path one takes toward achieving holistic health and well-being.

The healing journey through somatic therapy is grounded in the principle of neuroplasticity—the brain's remarkable ability to reorganize itself by forming new connections throughout life. Engaging in somatic practices such as mindful movement, breathwork, and grounding techniques can facilitate this neural reorganization, gradually diminishing the intensity of trauma responses and fostering a sense of safety in the body. These practices encourage activating the parasympathetic nervous system, counteracting the body's stress response, and promoting relaxation and healing.

Furthermore, directing attention to bodily sensations in a nonjudgmental manner helps to rewire the brain's perception of threat, gradually shifting from a state of constant vigilance to one of presence and calm. This shift not only alleviates the somatic symptoms of trauma but also enables individuals to reclaim a sense of control over their bodies and emotions, a pivotal step in the journey toward healing.

ception undermines the inclusive spirit of somatic therapy, which adapts to meet each individual where they are, regardless of their physical condition or experience with body-centered practices. The essence of somatic treatment lies in its capacity to attune to the subtle languages of the body, guiding individuals toward greater self-awareness and embodiment through gentle, accessible exercises.

Therapy Limitations

In acknowledging the strengths of somatic therapy, it is equally important to recognize its limitations. Somatic therapy, like any therapeutic modality, is not a one-size-fits-all solution. Its effectiveness is influenced by several factors, including the individual's readiness to engage with body-centered practices, the nature of their psychological concerns, and the quality of the therapeutic relationship. Also, somatic therapy may not be suitable for individuals with certain medical conditions that limit their ability to participate in physical exercises, underscoring the need for a thorough assessment and personalized approach.

Managing expectations becomes a crucial aspect of the therapeutic process, ensuring that individuals approach somatic therapy with a clear understanding of its potential and its boundaries. This transparency fosters a realistic perspective, allowing individuals to engage with the treatment in a way that honors their unique path to healing.

Integrative Approaches

One of somatic therapy's greatest strengths lies in its capacity to integrate seamlessly with other therapeutic modalities, creating a holistic approach to healing that encompasses mind, body, and spirit. By incorporating somatic practices into cognitive-behavioral therapy, psychoanalysis, or art therapy, therapists can offer a more comprehensive treatment plan that addresses the complex nature of psychological distress.

This integrative approach recognizes the psychological and bodily interconnectedness, acknowledging that emotional healing cannot be fully realized without attending to the body. It offers individuals a diverse toolkit, equipping them with the resources to navigate their healing journey with flexibility and depth. Integrating various modalities allows for a flexible and adaptable approach to promoting psychological well-being, surpassing its limitations.

In somatic therapy, myths are dispelled through experience, through the tangible shifts that occur when individuals begin to listen to the wisdom of their bodies. The evidence supporting its efficacy continues to grow, grounded in scientific research and personal narratives of transformation. While acknowledging its limitations, somatic therapy maintains its humility and considers the unique needs and journeys of those it aims to help.

Somatic Therapy vs. Traditional Psychotherapy

A Comparative Analysis

Somatic therapy and traditional psychotherapy are distinct yet complementary paths. By integrating various approaches, a complex healing tapestry is woven that respects the intricacy of the human experience. This invites a more comprehensive and holistic journey toward achieving wellness.

Comparative Framework

At first glance, somatic therapy and traditional psychotherapy diverge significantly in method and focus. Traditional psychotherapy, with its roots deeply entrenched in the exploration of thoughts, feelings, and the subconscious, often unfolds in the realm of conversation. It seeks to untangle the psychological knots of the past and present, primarily through dialogue and cognitive understanding. In contrast, somatic therapy shifts the spotlight to the body as a gateway to unearthing and healing emotional wounds. It assumes that the body holds onto trauma and stress, manifesting in physical symptoms and patterns that, when engaged with awareness and compassion, can lead to profound emotional release and insight.

Yet, beneath these methodological differences lies a shared commitment to holistic healing. Both approaches recognize the connection between mind and body, acknowledging that true healing necessitates attention to both.

Where traditional psychotherapy excels in articulating and reframing cognitive and emotional patterns, somatic therapy offers a tangible, experiential path to accessing and transforming these patterns through the body. Together, they encompass a spectrum of therapeutic engagement, from the abstract to the tangible, from thought to sensation.

★Integrative Potential

Integration is the process of incorporating new insights and experiences into one's understanding and behavior.

The real magic unfolds when somatic therapy and traditional psychotherapy converge, creating a symbiotic relationship that enriches the therapeutic experience. Integrating somatic practices into traditional psychotherapy sessions can deepen the client's self-awareness, grounding abstract emotional insights into the body's physical experiences. This integration offers clients a dual pathway to healing, enabling them to explore their internal landscapes through conversation and bodily sensation. It fosters a more embodied form of insight, where cognitive understanding and somatic awareness inform and amplify each other.

For therapists trained in both modalities, this integrated approach allows for a fluid, responsive engagement with clients, tailoring sessions to meet the individual's needs in the moment. Whether through a guided body scan that brings a client back to the present or a discussion that lends language to a previously unspoken bodily sensation, the healing potential expands exponentially when the wisdom of both somatic therapy and traditional psychotherapy are used simultaneously.

Client Experiences

The impact of this integrative approach is perhaps most vividly reflected in clients' experiences. Those who have navigated the waters of both somatic therapy and traditional psychotherapy often report a more rounded, grounded sense of healing. Where traditional psychotherapy provides the map, somatic therapy offers the terrain, inviting clients to step into the landscape of their experiences with all their senses engaged.

Clients recounted moments of revelation when a shift in posture unveiled a long-buried emotion or when a deep, mindful breath illuminated a path through anxiety. These experiences, rooted in the body, often provide the missing pieces to the puzzles explored in traditional psychotherapy sessions. Thus, the narrative of healing becomes a more vivid, multisensory story, one where insights are not just understood but felt, lived, and embodied.

Therapeutic Goals

While the methods may differ, somatic therapy and traditional psychotherapy converge to foster healing, growth, and a more harmonious relationship with oneself. Both seek to alleviate suffering, whether in the mind, the body, or the intricate dance between the two. They strive to empower individuals with the tools and awareness to navigate life's challenges with resilience and grace.

Yet, their approach to these goals illuminates different facets of the human experience. Traditional psychotherapy often focuses on the narrative of the self, exploring stories, beliefs, and patterns that shape one's world experience. On the other hand, somatic therapy anchors this narrative in the physical body, exploring how these stories and patterns are held, expressed, and potentially transformed through bodily awareness.

This distinction does not imply a hierarchy but rather a complementary relationship, where each approach enriches the other. By engaging both the cognitive and the somatic, therapists can offer a more holistic path to healing that honors the complexity and depth of the human experience.

In the end, the choice between somatic therapy and traditional psychotherapy—or the decision to weave them together—is deeply personal, reflecting the individual's needs, preferences, and journey toward healing. What remains constant is the potential for transformation, a testament to the power of engaging with the full spectrum of our being, from the depths of our psyche to the wisdom of our bodies.

Chapter 1: Tools and Techniques

Embodiment

- Body scanning

- Journaling

Chapter 2

Breathing Life into Healing

Key Practices in Somatic Therapy

Within the rich diversity of existence, breath is the most unassuming yet profound rhythm, weaving moments of life together in a continuous flow. Often overlooked, this gentle tide within us holds the power to transform turmoil into tranquility. This chapter delves into the essence of breath as a tool for healing, not through grand gestures but through the simplicity of being and breathing. Here, we explore how breathing, something intrinsic to life, can become a deliberate practice of healing and transformation.

The Power of Breath: Oxygen as Medicine

★ Breathwork

Breathwork is a technique that uses breathing exercises to improve mental, physical, and spiritual well-being.

Breathwork in somatic therapy encompasses various techniques, each with its own unique rhythm and purpose.

- **Diaphragmatic Breathing**: Focus on the rise and fall of your belly during each inhalation and exhalation.

- **The 4-7-8 Technique**: Inhale for four counts, holding for seven, and exhaling for eight promotes a state of calm.

- **Alternate Nostril Breathing**: A practice borrowed from ancient yoga traditions, balancing the body's energies and aligning the emotional state with a sense of centeredness.

  - Close your eyes and take a few deep breaths through both nostrils, allowing your body to relax.

  - With your right hand, bring your index finger and middle finger to rest between your eyebrows (using your third finger to block your left nostril and your thumb to block your right nostril).

  - After a few breaths, close your right nostril with your right thumb and inhale deeply through your left nostril.

  - At the top of your inhale, close your left nostril with your right ring finger, release your right nostril, and exhale fully through your right nostril.

  - Inhale deeply through your right nostril.

  - At the top of your inhale, close your right nostril with your right thumb again, release your left nostril, and exhale fully through your left nostril.

  - Continue this pattern, alternating nostrils with each inhale and exhale. Inhale through one nostril, switch, and exhale through the other nostril.

  - Continue for several rounds, focusing on the flow of breath and maintaining a steady rhythm.

  - After completing several rounds, release your hand and return to normal breathing. Take a moment to notice any changes in your body and mind.

While distinct, each technique shares a common thread—they all harness the breath to navigate the body's responses to stress and trauma, offering a direct line to the autonomic nervous system. Individuals learn to modulate their physiological state by engaging with these practices, shifting from distress to emotional balance.

Physiological Effects

The impact of breathwork on the physical body is profound and multifaceted. At their core, breathwork practices engage the parasympathetic nervous system—the rest and digest counterpoint to the body's fight-or-flight responses. This engagement signals the body to slow the heart rate, lower blood pressure, and promote physiological relaxation. It's like turning the dial on a radio from a station of static and noise to one of clear, soothing melodies.

Scientific investigations into the physiological effects of breathwork reveal significant reductions in stress markers, including cortisol levels. This suggests a tangible, measurable impact on the body's stress response mechanisms. This evidence underscores breathwork's role not merely as a practice of the mind but as a deeply embodied technique for wellness.

Practice Guidelines

For those new to breathwork, the practice might seem daunting, cloaked in a veil of mystique. Yet, the beauty of breathwork lies in its accessibility. Begin with a simple commitment to observe your breath, noting its quality and rhythm without judgment.

Experiment with structured techniques from this place of awareness, starting with diaphragmatic breathing.

A quiet, comfortable space free from the distractions of daily life supports this practice.

- **Dedicate a few minutes daily to breathwork.**

As with any practice, consistency is vital. Make it a sanctuary of calm in your routine. Regular engagement with breathwork deepens its impact, embedding a sense of calm into the core of one's being.

The 4-7-8 breathing technique has saved me time and time again from becoming overwhelmed by anxiety. This practice, integrated into moments of escalating stress, becomes a lifeline, a tool to reclaim a sense of control amid the chaos of anxiety.

I had the chance to share a couple of experiences with a veteran grappling with PTSD. His name is Denis. He shared with me that, for him, nostril breathing has become a bridge to peace, a way to navigate the traumatic memories with a newfound sense of balance.

Breath, in its simplicity, carries within it the seeds of transformation—a reminder that healing often begins not with grand gestures but with the quiet, deliberate practice of being present with ourselves. Through the techniques explored in this chapter, we find methods to soothe the physiological echoes of stress and trauma and a path to reconnect with the rhythmic essence of life itself.

Creating a Safe Space for Somatic Work

In somatic therapy, the environment in which one practices holds as much significance as the practice itself. The physical and emotional setting acts as a crucible for the beautiful transformation. Therefore, it is imperative to cultivate spaces that facilitate and enhance the therapeutic journey. Creating a conducive environment extends beyond the arrangement of physical elements; it encompasses fostering emotional safety, establishing boundaries and consent, and nurturing support systems that collectively support a secure somatic experience.

Physical Environment

The physical space for somatic work, whether a professional therapy room or a corner of one's home, demands careful consideration and intentionality in its design. Such spaces evoke a sense of sanctuary, a retreat from external distractions where one can easily turn inward. Elements such as soft, indirect lighting, serene color palettes, and natural components like plants or water features can significantly alter the ambiance, rendering it conducive to relaxation and introspection. The setup should facilitate unrestricted movement, which is crucial for somatic practices. It should also come with privacy provisions that prevent any intrusion from the outside world. In creating this environment, one crafts a setting that supports and amplifies the healing process, making physical space an active participant in the somatic journey.

Emotional Safety

Beyond the tangible, the intangible atmosphere of emotional safety is a cornerstone of practical somatic work. This encompasses a space where vulnerabilities can surface without fear of judgment, where emotions can flow freely, and where the individual feels seen and heard in their entirety. Achieving this necessitates an unwavering presence and empathy from the therapist or facilitator and an explicit acknowledgment of the space as a judgment-free zone. Techniques such as active listening, validation of feelings, and the gentle guidance of somatic exploration without pushing beyond comfort zones are pivotal. In cultivating such an atmosphere, one lays the groundwork for trust and openness, essential ingredients for deep, transformative work.

Boundaries and Consent

At the heart of somatic therapy lies the principle of autonomy, underscored by clearly defined boundaries and the paramount importance of consent. This is particularly vital given the therapy's inherent physicality, whether in movements or therapist-guided touch, should it form part of the practice. Establishing boundaries begins with an open dialogue about the individual's comfort levels. It continues with ongoing check-ins to ensure these thresholds are respected. Consent, similarly, is not a one-time agreement but a continuous process where the individual's autonomy to pause, alter, or cease the practice at any point is unequivocally upheld. Such practices maintain a safe, respectful space, allowing the individual to engage fully with the therapeutic process without apprehension.

Support Systems

The journey through somatic therapy, marked by moments of vulnerability and revelation, is not to be undertaken in isolation. The fabric of support, woven from relationships within and beyond the therapeutic setting, plays a critical role in sustaining and enriching the individual's experience. Within the therapy room, this might manifest as a collaboration between therapist and client, a partnership in which the client's insights and experiences are valued and built upon. Beyond that, it involves cultivating a network—friends, family, or peer groups—who can offer understanding, encouragement, and a listening ear. Additionally, resources such as reading materials, online forums, or community workshops can provide further support, offering diverse perspectives and collective wisdom. Together, these systems of support act as a scaffold around the individual, offering strength, perspective, and a sense of belonging throughout their somatic journey.

In sum, creating a safe space for somatic work is a multifaceted endeavor that requires attentiveness, intention, and care. It is about constructing an environment that shelters and nurtures. In this setting, the body can speak and be heard, emotions can surface and find expression, and the individual can traverse the depths of their inner world with assurance and safety. Through the interplay of physical ambiance, emotional safety, boundaries, consent, and support systems, we lay the foundations for a therapeutic journey that is as secure as it is profound.

Grounding Techniques for Immediate Relief

★ Grounding

Grounding is a technique to return to the present moment and reconnect with the physical body.

In somatic therapy, grounding is a pivotal technique, bridging the emotional or sensory overwhelm vortex to the present moment. Grounding draws upon the body's inherent capacity to connect with here-and-now realities, facilitating a re-anchoring of the self in the face of disquieting thoughts or feelings.

It leverages the tangible—the sensation of the fabric against skin, the solidity of the earth beneath one's feet, or the rhythmic cadence of one's breath—to foster an immediate sense of stability and centeredness. This method proves indispensable within therapeutic contexts, serving as a tool for therapists to guide clients through moments of distress and as a self-administered technique for individuals seeking comfort amid daily commotion.

The spectrum of grounding techniques offers a rich tableau, each method tailored to engage different senses and accommodate diverse needs and preferences.

The following structured sensory journey effectively diverts attention from distressing stimuli, reorienting focus toward immediate sensory experiences.

- **The "5-4-3-2-1" Technique**: Identify five (5) things you can see, four (4) you can touch, three (3) you can hear, two (2) you can smell, and one (1) you can taste. Write them in your journal.

This next technique allows the mind to find a respite from anxiety or disconnection, fostering a palpable sense of grounding.

- **The "Object Focus" Technique**: Choose an object—a stone, a piece of jewelry, or any item with personal significance—and direct your attention to its texture, temperature, and weight.

For those who find solace in movement, the following practice entails a conscious focus. It cultivates a moving meditation, uniting body and mind in walking and thus grounding the individual in physical sensation and locomotion.

- **The "Walking Mindfulness" Technique**: While walking, focus on the sensations experienced with each step—the feel of the ground through the soles, the rhythm of movement, and the interplay of balance and motion.

When to Use

Knowing when to use grounding techniques depends on being highly aware of your internal feelings and recognizing when you're starting to feel overwhelmed emotionally or physically, which signals that it's time to take action.

These techniques are particularly potent when the disconnection between mind and body becomes pronounced, for example:

- Anxiety spikes

- Flashbacks

- Dissociative episodes

They are also beneficial in everyday scenarios marked by stress or agitation, for example:

- In anticipation of a challenging event

- In the aftermath of an unsettling interaction

- In the hustle of daily life

The key lies in preemptive recognition and timely application, transforming grounding from a reactive measure to a proactive strategy for emotional regulation and presence.

Self-Help Strategies

Empowering individuals to self-administer grounding techniques underscores the essence of somatic therapy, fostering autonomy and resilience.

- **Create a "Grounding Kit":** Fill a kit with sensory objects (smooth stones, aromatic oils, tactile fabrics) that offer a tangible resource that individuals can draw upon.

- **Maintain a Grounding Journal:** Document the efficacy of different techniques in various contexts, thereby honing a personalized repertoire of strategies. This can serve as a reflective tool.

- **Establish a Daily Routine for Grounding:** This can be done through morning "object focus" meditations or evening "walking mindfulness." Include brief, periodic grounding checks throughout the day, such as pausing to take three conscious breaths or pressing one's feet firmly into the ground.

This cultivates a centeredness baseline, reducing the effects of potential stressors.

Embedding these techniques into your daily life ensures they are readily available when needed.

In essence, grounding techniques offer a versatile and immediate avenue for reconnecting with the present moment, leveraging the body's sensory experiences as anchors in the seas of emotional and sensory overwhelm.

These techniques provide a lifeline to stability and centeredness through varied methods tailored to individual preferences and contexts. By fostering awareness of internal cues and integrating grounding into daily practices, individuals equip themselves with a powerful toolkit for navigating the challenges of both the therapeutic setting and the broader landscape of life's stresses. In doing so, grounding emerges as a technique and a fundamental aspect of a balanced, present-oriented approach to well-being, reinforcing the body's role as a sanctuary of stability and a conduit for healing.

The Power of Mindfulness in Somatic Practice

★ Mindfulness

Mindfulness is the practice of maintaining a moment-by-moment awareness of our thoughts, feelings, and bodily sensations.

At its core, mindfulness encapsulates a state of active, open attention to the present. Far from a passive encounter with the moment, it entails a conscious direction of awareness toward the here and now, observing thoughts, feelings, and sensations without judgment. This practice, rooted in ancient traditions, has found its place in modern somatic therapy as a powerful ally, augmenting healing through an enriched connection with oneself.

Mindfulness and the Body

Mindfulness intertwines with bodily awareness in an intricate dance of consciousness, where each step into the realm of the present moment deepens one's connection with the physical self. The body, often relegated to the backdrop of our daily experiences, emerges into the spotlight under the gaze of mindfulness. This union of mind and body awareness fosters a dialogue where the body's subtle signals of discomfort or ease become messages to be acknowledged and understood. The technique of scanning one's body, often employed within mindfulness disciplines, bridges this dialogue, allowing for a systematic exploration of physical sensations. Through this method, the subtle tensions held within the body's memory of past traumas or the flutter of anxiety in the belly are observed, truly felt, and recognized, marking the first steps toward healing.

Integrating Mindfulness

Incorporating mindfulness into somatic therapy sessions transforms these encounters into a deeply immersive experience. Therapists may initiate a session by guiding clients through a mindfulness exercise, focusing on the breath, or conducting a body scan. This immersion in the present moment sets the foundation for the session, creating a conducive space for deeper somatic exploration.

Beyond these guided practices, therapists encourage clients to be mindful of their interactions with their physical sensations throughout therapy.

- **Notice the changes in your breath during moments of emotional revelation.**

- **Observe the bodily sensations that accompany recollections of past events.**

Such integration of mindfulness enhances the therapeutic process. It equips clients with skills that transcend the therapy room, seeping into their daily lives.

Mindfulness Benefits

Incorporating mindfulness into somatic therapy unfurls many benefits, touching various facets of well-being resilience.

On a foundational level, this practice:

- Cultivates an enhanced state of relaxation, countering the body's stress responses with a gentle but potent calm force.

- Improves the ability to regulate emotions, a skill rooted in the heightened awareness of their emotional states and how these are mirrored in their bodies.

- Provides a greater capacity for dealing with physical or emotional pain, as mindfulness fosters an attitude of acceptance. Under the mindfulness lens, pain is observed and acknowledged without the added layer of resistance that often amplifies suffering.

- Nurtures resilience, arming clients with the ability to face life's adversities with a composed and grounded disposition. This resilience is born from the practice of returning to the present moment, a skill that, once honed, becomes an anchor amid the storms of stress or trauma.

- Provides an enriched sense of connection with oneself, a bond strengthened by attentive listening to their bodies' needs and messages. This internal connection paves the way for a more compassionate self-relationship, where judgments give way to understanding and kindness.

- Fosters openness and curiosity, enriching communication and deepening connections.

The ripple effects of mindfulness in somatic therapy also extend into interpersonal relationships. Armed with a deeper understanding of their emotional and physical states, clients navigate their interactions with others with greater empathy and patience.

In the practice of mindfulness within somatic therapy, the present moment becomes a canvas on which the journey of healing is painted. Through the intertwining of mind and body awareness, clients discover a path that alleviates immediate distress and lasting changes in their relationship with themselves and the world around them. This journey, marked by moments of profound insight and transformation, underscores the power of mindfulness as a therapeutic tool and a way of life—a practice that, once embraced, continues to unfold its benefits, layer by delicate layer, long after the therapy session has ended.

Understanding and Practicing Self-Compassion

In the nuanced sphere of somatic therapy, the cultivation of self-compassion emerges as a profound, yet often overlooked, element crucial for deep healing. This practice is an act of strength that fosters resilience, empathy, and a profound connection to oneself. It involves treating oneself with the same kindness, concern, and support one would offer a good friend. However, the path to embracing self-compassion is fraught with obstacles, shaped by cultural narratives that often equate self-kindness with selfishness or self-pity. Yet, overcoming these barriers is essential. The journey toward healing is as much about transforming our relationship with ourselves as it is about addressing our somatic experiences.

Self-Compassion in Therapy

In the therapeutic space, self-compassion becomes a pivotal tool, illuminating the path to healing with its gentle light. This process begins with a shift in perspective, where clients are encouraged to view their struggles through a lens of kindness and understanding rather than judgment and criticism. Such a shift is cognitive and deeply somatic, as clients learn to attune to their bodies with an attitude of care and acceptance. The body, with its history of pain, trauma, and neglect, is no longer an adversary but a cherished companion on the path to wellness. Therapists play a crucial role in facilitating this shift, modeling self-compassion through their interactions and providing a safe space where clients can explore their internal dialogues and somatic experiences without fear of judgment.

Barriers to Self-Compassion

Despite its undeniable value, self-compassion is often hindered by deeply ingrained beliefs and societal norms that valorize self-criticism and stigmatize self-care. Many individuals grapple with an internal critic that relentlessly questions their worthiness of compassion, a voice shaped by past experiences, cultural messages, and societal expectations. Overcoming these barriers requires a deliberate and often challenging process of unlearning, where individuals learn to question and counteract the critical voices with evidence of their inherent worth. This endeavor is supported by somatic practices that ground these new narratives in the body, allowing clients to understand their value and viscerally feel it intellectually.

Exercises for Growth

Specific exercises facilitate self-compassion growth, integrating this practice into daily life.

- **The Compassionate Touch:** Place your hands over your heart or other comforting parts of your body, focusing on the warmth and pressure of your touch.

This simple act serves as a bodily anchor for feelings of compassion, offering immediate comfort and a tangible reminder of your capacity for self-care.

- **The Self-Compassion Break:** Take a moment to pause amid the day's challenges to acknowledge your suffering, extend kindness to yourself, and remember the common humanity that connects us all in our imperfections.

When practiced regularly, these exercises become more than just actions—they become a natural part of how people see themselves and handle life.

Therapeutic Benefits

Integrating self-compassion into somatic therapy offers many therapeutic benefits, profoundly transforming the journey toward healing.

Clients who cultivate self-compassion:

- Report a significant decrease in negative emotions, a shift attributed to their newfound ability to meet their pain with kindness rather than resistance.

- Enhance their capacity for managing stress and anxiety as individuals learn to soothe themselves in moments of distress.

- Foster a stronger sense of connectedness with oneself and others, mitigating feelings of isolation and loneliness.

- Ensure a healthier, more nurturing internal dialogue, influencing how individuals approach their therapeutic work and daily lives.

- Lay the groundwork for sustained healing and personal growth.

- Build a resilient foundation upon which individuals can create a life marked by wellness, fulfillment, and deep, unwavering kindness toward themselves.

The practice of self-compassion stands as a beacon, guiding us toward a relationship with ourselves marked by kindness, understanding, and unconditional support. It teaches us that healing is not just about addressing the wounds of the past but about how we accompany ourselves in the present, with all our vulnerabilities and strengths. In this light, self-compassion emerges not as a luxury but as a necessity, a vital component of the therapeutic process that enriches our journey toward wholeness. As we transition from exploring the foundational practices of somatic therapy, let's carry forward the lessons of self-compassion, allowing them to illuminate our path as we dive deeper into the transformative potential of somatic work.

Chapter 2: Tools and Techniques

Breathing Techniques

- Diaphragmatic breathing

- 4-7-8 technique

- Alternate nostril breathing

Grounding Techniques & Tools

- 5-4-3-2-1 technique

- Object focus technique

- Walking mindfulness technique

- Create a grounding kit

- Maintain a grounding journal

- Establish a daily routine for grounding

Mindfulness Practice

- Notice the changes in your breath during the moments of emotional revelation.

- Observe the bodily sensations that accompany recollections of past events.

Self-Compassion Practice

- The compassionate touch

- The self-compassion break

Chapter 3

Embracing Somatics

From Awareness to Daily Practice

When the world hovers in a half-awake stillness before dawn, an opportunity exists for a profound connection with oneself. The body whispers its secrets in these early hours, telling tales of tension, resilience, and untapped potential. Here, in the nascent light of day, lies a metaphor for the initial steps into somatic awareness—a field ripe with the promise of discovery yet demanding gentle patience and keen observation to truly understand its language. As one learns to listen to these subtle bodily cues, a map of self-awareness begins to unfold, charting a course toward more profound connection and healing.

Enhancing somatic awareness is like learning a new language, where the body communicates through sensations rather than words. This attunement process is not instantaneous but evolves through practice, curiosity, and an openness to the messages conveyed through muscle, breath, and movement. To embark on this venture is to commit to a dialogue with oneself, fostering a relationship that thrives on attentiveness and nurturance.

Assessing Your Somatic Awareness

□ **Somatic Awareness**

Somatic awareness is the conscious perception of one's own body and bodily sensations.

The first step in enhancing somatic awareness is to:

- **Establish a Baseline:** Gain a clear understanding of your current level of connection with your body.

This initial assessment is like standing at the edge of a vast landscape, taking in the view before setting off to explore.

Simple questions can guide this exploration:

- How often do you notice tension in your body without an external prompt?

- Can you identify emotions based on physical sensations?

- Do you recognize when your breathing changes in response to stress or excitement?

These inquiries illuminate the relationship between mind and body, offering insights into areas ripe for development.

Tools for Assessment

Dedicate time to the following specific practices to enhance body mindfulness such as:

- **Body Scanning:** By lying still, closing your eyes, and directing your attention to each part of your body, you learn to notice the sensations that dwell within—tension, warmth, discomfort, or ease.

- **Mindful Movement Exercises:** Yoga or qi gong.

- **Breathwork:** Different options are provided in Chapter 2. This will help you foster a closer relationship with your respiratory patterns.

Incorporating these practices into daily routines, perhaps during those quiet moments before dawn or in the reflective pause before sleep, embeds somatic awareness into the rhythm of life, transforming it from an exercise into an embodied way of being.

As one progresses in these practices, periodic reassessment using the initial tools can offer feedback on growth, shedding light on the evolving dialogue between mind and body. This ongoing assessment, practice, and reassessment process forms the backbone of the journey into bodily awareness, a path marked by continuous discovery and deepening connection.

Through this detailed exploration of assessing somatic awareness, we embark on the first steps of a profoundly personal voyage into self-discovery. This journey invites a transformation that transcends the physical, weaving into the very essence of how we engage with ourselves and the world. As we move forward, let us carry the lessons of attentiveness, patience, and curiosity, allowing them to guide us toward a more integrated and harmonious existence.

Simple Somatic Exercises for Beginners

The initiation into the realm of somatic practices unfolds with an invitation to engage in accessible yet deeply transformative exercises. These activities, designed with the novice in mind, are the initial steps toward cultivating a profound connection between mind and body. They are simple in their execution but rich in their capacity to foster awareness and presence.

To begin this exploration into somatic exercises:

- **Acknowledge your Current State of Being:** Invite a moment of stillness, a pause in the day's rhythm, to be with yourself. This initial step is crucial, setting the tone for a practice grounded in self-awareness and attentiveness.

- **Find a Quiet Space:** Ensure that interruptions are minimized to encourage a sense of privacy and focus.

- **Adopt a Supportive and Comfortable Posture:** You can sit, stand, or lie down.

The essence of this starting point is to foster an environment where the individual feels at ease and can direct their attention inward without strain.

For those at the beginning of their somatic journey, consistency and moderation are vital elements in integrating these practices into daily life. Beginners are recommended to dedicate a few minutes daily to their somatic exercises, gradually increasing the duration as they grow comfortable and familiar with the practices.

A starting point might be five minutes of focused breath awareness or a body scan, expanding to ten or fifteen minutes as the individual finds their rhythm.

One foundational exercise is often recommended for those new to somatic practices.

- **The Mindful Body Scan**: Close your eyes and take a few deep breaths to center yourself. Starting at the crown of the head, attention is gently guided down through the body, pausing at each area—forehead, jaw, shoulders, arms, hands, torso, hips, legs, feet—to notice any sensations present. Tension, warmth, tingling, or perhaps the absence of sensation are all observed without judgment.

The key is to approach this exploration with curiosity, allowing whatever arises to be acknowledged.

If areas of tightness are encountered:

- **Soften Tight Spaces:** Imagine your breath flowing into and softening these spaces, promoting relaxation and release.

Another exercise that proves beneficial for beginners:

- **Focused Breath Awareness:** Place a hand on the abdomen, feeling the rise and fall with each breath.

This tactile connection enhances the awareness of the breath's natural rhythm, grounding the individual in the present moment. The simplicity of this exercise is powerful in keeping the mind and body in a shared experience, fostering a harmonious state of being.

The objective is not to adhere to a rigid schedule but to allow the practice to naturally find its place within the ebb and flow of daily routines. This gentle approach ensures that the exercises enrich rather than overwhelm, becoming a source of grounding and presence rather than another task on the day's agenda.

Expected Outcomes

Regular engagement with these somatic exercises unveils many benefits, even for those beginning their practice.

People often report:

- A heightened sense of bodily awareness, noticing sensations they previously overlooked. This increased sensitivity fosters a deeper connection with oneself, illuminating the body's wisdom and its capacity to signal needs, emotions, and boundaries.

- An enhanced ability to manage stress, as these exercises equip them with tools to ground themselves in moments of overwhelm, cultivating calm amid chaos and offering immediate relief.

- Improvements in their concentration and presence, finding themselves more fully engaged in the tasks and interactions of their daily lives. This stems from the mindfulness inherent in somatic practices, which trains the mind to remain anchored in the present, attentive to the richness of each moment.

- A more compassionate relationship with oneself, as observing the body without judgment, extends to a broader acceptance of one's experiences and emotions.

The journey into somatic practices begins with simple but profound steps, leading the individual toward enhanced awareness, presence, and harmony within themselves. Through regular engagement with these foundational exercises, beginners unlock the door to a richer, more attuned experience of their bodies and lives, setting the stage for continued exploration and growth in somatic awareness.

Overcoming Skepticism: Trusting the Process

Addressing Doubts

Skepticism toward somatic therapy often emerges from unfamiliarity, where the tangible intertwines with the intangible, and the scientific meets the experiential. At this intersection, doubts take root, questioning the efficacy of a therapy that leans into the body's wisdom to foster emotional and psychological healing. To address these doubts, it begins with an open dialogue that acknowledges the skepticism and invites it into the conversation. This involves presenting somatic therapy not as an alternative to traditional mental health treatments but as a complementary approach that enhances overall well-being by tapping into the body's inherent capacity for healing. Educating skeptics about the grounding in neuroscience—how the therapy influences the nervous system, alters brain activity associated with stress and trauma, and promotes emotional regulation—can demystify the process, bridging the gap between doubt and understanding.

The dialogue extends to the experiential, encouraging skeptics to engage in simple somatic exercises, allowing them to witness firsthand the subtle yet profound shifts when attention is directed toward bodily sensations. This firsthand experience is a powerful counter to skepticism, providing a tangible touchstone for understanding the therapy's benefits. Through these small, personal revelations, the walls of doubt crumble, replaced by curiosity and openness toward the somatic journey.

Building Trust

Much like the therapy itself, trust in the somatic process unfolds from within, nurtured by experiences that validate the body's role as a conduit for healing. Building this trust involves creating a space of safety and acceptance where individuals feel empowered to explore their bodily sensations without fear of judgment or expectation. This requires patience, both by the therapist and the individual, as trust is not demanded but gently cultivated over time. It's in the repeated moments of connection between bodily sensations and emotional insights that trust in the process solidifies, each experience reinforcing the validity and value of the somatic approach.

The therapist's role in this is paramount, embodying a presence that exudes empathy, authenticity, and unwavering support. They serve as guides, their expertise, and confidence in the somatic method acting as steady beacons that light the way through moments of uncertainty. Incorporating feedback loops, where individuals reflect on their experiences, noting shifts in their emotional landscape, physical sensations, and overall well-being, reinforces trust. These reflections are evidence of the therapy's impact, tangible markers of progress bolstering confidence in the somatic path.

When someone can find a sense of closure that had eluded them for years by unearthing and processing long-held grief, and another can discover a wellspring of creativity and confidence that transformed their approach to life and relationships, these success stories invite skeptics to see beyond their doubts. They also foster a sense of community, a realization that one's struggles and aspirations echo the experiences of others, providing both comfort and inspiration.

Patience and Commitment

With its depths and complexities, the somatic journey demands patience and commitment, qualities that serve as the bedrock for overcoming skepticism. This path does not promise quick fixes but unfolds gradually, revealing its gifts to those who engage with openness and perseverance. Patience is cultivated through practice, as individuals learn to sit with their experiences without rushing to judgment or immediate resolution. It's in this space of allowing that true healing begins as the body and mind synchronize in a dance of discovery and understanding.

Commitment to the process is a declaration of trust in somatic therapy and oneself. It's a commitment to exploration, to the belief that within the body lies the knowledge and power to heal. This dedication, supported by the therapist's guidance and the collective wisdom of those who have walked this path, anchors the individual in their journey, providing the strength to navigate the challenges and embrace the transformations.

As one builds trust in somatic therapy, the path unfolds with clarity and purpose, guided by education, personal experience, and the resonant power of shared stories. Doubts are addressed, trust is nurtured, and a commitment to the journey is fortified, leading to healing and self-discovery.

Incorporating Somatic Practices into Daily Life

Integrating somatic practices into the rhythm of daily existence demands a nuanced approach that respects individual schedules while ensuring that these vital exercises are preserved in the shuffle of obligations. The key lies in weaving these practices into our routines, making them as integral as morning coffee or brushing teeth, thus ensuring their transformation from optional activities to indispensable elements of well-being.

Daily Integration

Adapting somatic practices for daily integration begins with an honest assessment of one's daily patterns, identifying moments that naturally lend themselves to a pause, a breath, or a movement. It might be the tranquility accompanying the first light of dawn, the lull that follows lunch, or the solitude of the evening hours. Somatic exercises can be gently introduced into these spaces, starting with a minute of focused breathing or a brief body scan. Over time, these moments can be expanded, evolving into comprehensive practices that stand as pillars of one's day. The aim is not to carve out a lot of time but to find and utilize small pockets of availability, ensuring that somatic practices become threads in the tapestry of daily life.

Creating Habits

Cultivating somatic exercises into habitual components of our lives requires understanding habit formation. Key to this process is the principle of consistency, coupled with the power of cues and rewards. The association strengthens by attaching somatic practices to established routines—such as performing a series of mindful stretches before showering or engaging in a grounding exercise before meals—reinforcing the habit. Rewards play a crucial role, too; they don't have to be external but can stem from the practice itself—the sense of calm after a breathing exercise, the release following a stretch. Acknowledging and savoring these intrinsic rewards fortifies the desire to continue knitting somatic practices into the continuum of daily actions.

Overcoming Challenges

Challenges invariably arise while maintaining a regular somatic practice, from time constraints to competing priorities. Overcoming these hurdles first demands acknowledgment, recognizing that fluctuations in practice are part of the process rather than indicators of failure.

Flexibility becomes a vital ally, allowing for adaptation in the face of obstacles.

Can a morning practice be woven into the evening routine if missed?

If time is scarce, might a few mindful breaths serve in place of a longer session?

This adaptive approach ensures that somatic practices remain fluid, capable of morphing to fit the contours of changing circumstances. Also, cultivating a supportive community—through virtual platforms, local groups, or participation in workshops—can provide motivation and accountability, keeping the commitment to somatic practice vibrant, even when individual resolve wavers.

Long-Term Benefits

The long-term benefits of consistent somatic practice reveal themselves subtly, manifesting in layers that deepen over time.

People have reported:

- A noticeable enhancement in bodily awareness, a sharpening of the senses that tunes individuals into the whispers of their physical form.

- A more intimate relationship with the body, where communication flows both ways, allows for the preemptive recognition of stress signals and the early adoption of coping strategies.

- The capacity for emotional regulation, with somatic practices offering a reliable conduit for the processing and releasing of emotional tension.

- A stronger immune system.

- Enhanced sleep quality.

- A reduction in the incidence of stress-related ailments.

- Improved concentration and productivity, enabling individuals to engage with their tasks and interactions with heightened presence and clarity.

- Overall health and well-being.

- Stronger interpersonal relationships result from heightened self-awareness and emotional regulation. Empathy and understanding are enhanced, fostering deeper connections with others. Individuals find themselves better equipped to navigate the complexities of communication, conflict, and connection, contributing to more harmonious and fulfilling relationships.

Integrating somatic practices into daily life is an exercise in discipline and a journey toward holistic well-being. It is a commitment that, while requiring patience and adaptability, offers profound rewards that permeate every aspect of existence.

Chapter 3: Tools and Techniques

Somatic Awareness

- Establish a baseline

Somatic Exercises for Beginners

- Acknowledge your current state of being

- Find a quiet space

- Adopt a comfortable and supportive posture

- Mindful body scan

- Soften tight spaces

- Focused breath awareness

Chapter 4

Navigating the Emotional Terrain

Somatic Practices for Understanding and Managing Responses

As we experience the highs and lows of our daily lives, our bodies act as conduits, navigating various emotions ranging from serenity to turmoil. During this time, somatic therapy's essence is a guiding light, illuminating the intricate dance between physical sensations and emotional states. Movement and mindfulness have the potential for profound understanding and transformation.

Emotional Awareness

At the heart of somatic therapy lies emotional awareness, the ability to recognize and name the emotions as they surface in the body. This awareness is like deciphering a map where emotions are landmarks, guiding us through our internal landscape. However, understanding this map requires attention and practice.

The body communicates its emotional state through sensations, for example:

- A tightness in the chest may speak of anxiety.

- A flutter in the stomach might signal excitement or fear.

Recognizing these signals is the first step in navigating the emotional tides within us.

Consider a scenario where a wave of sadness unexpectedly surges during a somatic exercise focused on releasing shoulder tension. This moment, though initially confusing, offers a profound opportunity for insight. It's the body's way of revealing stored emotions and asking for acknowledgment. This is where somatic therapy invites a pause, a breath, and a gentle exploration of this sadness, tracing its origins and understanding its presence.

Managing Intense Emotions

When somatic practices unearth intense emotions, the experience can be as challenging as enlightening. Strategies for managing these emotions are crucial, allowing for safe exploration without becoming overwhelmed.

Effective methods:

- **Grounding:** Focus on physical sensations that anchor you in the present, like the feel of the ground beneath your feet or the texture of the fabric in your hands.

- **Pendulation:** Imagine a gentle oscillation between the sensation of distress and a place of safety or neutrality in the body. The term is borrowed from somatic experiencing.

This approach prevents becoming stuck in intense emotional states, facilitating a gradual and manageable processing of emotions. (Explained in more detail in Chapter 6.)

Support Systems

The role of support systems in navigating emotional responses cannot be overstated. Whether composed of therapists, friends, family, or peer groups, these networks provide a safety net, offering validation, understanding, and perspective.

Sharing the experience of a somatic exercise that evoked unexpected emotions can demystify it and normalize the connection between physical sensations and emotional states.

Support systems also offer practical advice, from shared strategies for managing intense emotions to reminders of the importance of self-care and patience.

Self-Care Post-Exercise

Following somatic exercises that evoke strong emotions, self-care practices are essential.

These can range from:

- **Journaling:** Write down your thoughts and feelings, which allows for the processing and integration of the experience.

- **Comforting Physical Activities:** Walk, stretch, or take a warm bath.

The key is to listen to the body's needs, offering it kindness and care after the vulnerability of emotional exploration. For instance, after a session focused on releasing tension in the hips, which might unexpectedly release feelings of fear or sadness, taking time to wrap yourself in a cozy blanket and sip warm tea can be a soothing practice, honoring the body's journey through emotional release.

By understanding emotional awareness, employing strategies to manage intense emotions, leaning on support systems, and prioritizing self-care, individuals learn to navigate these waters with skill and compassion. This journey, rich with personal discoveries and challenges, underscores the transformative power of somatic practices in fostering emotional resilience and understanding.

Somatic Exercises for Specific Emotions

Anxiety

In somatic therapy, exercises tailored to address distinct emotions act as keys, unlocking doors to deeper understanding and managing these states.

Anxiety is a sensation often characterized by a quickened heartbeat and shallow breathing. Grounding exercises that emphasize connection to the earth provide a counterbalance, instilling a sense of calm and stability.

- **The "Earthing" Method:**

  - Stand barefoot on natural ground.

  - Visualize roots extending from the soles of the feet deep into the earth.

  - Take deep, slow breaths to enhance this connection. Each inhalation draws stability from the ground, and each exhalation releases the jittery energy of anxiety back into the earth.

Timing plays a pivotal role in the effectiveness of these exercises. For anxiety, the moments just before a known stressor—a meeting, a social event, or any situation that typically heightens one's sense of unease—are opportune times for "Earthing." This preemptive approach can establish a foundation of calm that underlies the ensuing activity. Alternatively, engaging in this practice at the end of the day allows for unwinding accumulated stress, grounding any lingering anxiety in preparation for rest.

- **Prepare Herbal Teas:** Use teas known for their calming properties, such as chamomile or lavender, to complement the grounding effect of "Earthing."

Sadness

Sadness may find solace in gentle, flowing movements that mimic water—reminding one of the transient nature of emotions.

The "Fluid Motion" exercise finds its moment in the quiet aftermath of a loss or disappointment when sadness's weight feels immediate and overwhelming. In the solitude of reflection, allowing the body to embody and release sadness can facilitate a gentle healing process.

- **The "Fluid Motion" Technique:**

  - Start seated or standing, and allow the body to sway gently, guided by the breath.

  - With each inhale, the body rises slightly; with each exhale, it softens, bends, and flows.

  - Eyes can be closed to turn the focus inward, inviting the emotion of sadness to express itself through the body's dance, acknowledging its presence, and letting it know it is free to leave.

- **Create Art:** Try painting, writing, or music to allow the emotions stirred by "Fluid Motion" to find expression in creative forms, facilitating a process of externalization and release.

Anger

Anger, a fiery companion that tightens the jaw and clenches the fists, might be met with exercises that channel this intense energy through vigorous activities like stomping or clapping, transforming it into a force for empowerment rather than destruction.

The following method offers a constructive outlet.

- **The "Dynamic Release" Method:**

  - Find a private space where you can safely express the intensity of your anger without reservation.

  - Begin with a solid and powerful stance and perform deliberate stompings with rhythmic hand clapping.

  - Each stomp and clap can be synchronized with a breath, the exhalations vocalizing a sound that resonates with the individual's current emotional state.

This physical expression of anger is not an act of violence but a declaration of one's right to feel and release emotion in a healthy and affirming manner. Engaging in the "Dynamic Release" exercise before the anger finds expression in less constructive ways can prevent the escalation of conflict, turning a potentially destructive emotion into a catalyst for personal strength.

Engaging in dialogue offers a path toward resolution and peace.

- **Engage in Dialogue:** Talk to a therapist, a trusted friend, or take time for self-reflection for an additional perspective on understanding the root causes of this emotion.

Complementary Practices

Enhancing the impact of these targeted exercises involves incorporating practices that support and extend their benefits.

Mindfulness meditation is a powerful ally to all three exercises. It instills a habit of presence, ensuring that the individual remains fully engaged with their emotional state and the sensations it evokes within the body.

- **Mindfulness Meditation:** Take slow, deep breaths and slow down racing thoughts by focusing on the breath.

Journaling offers a reflective space to articulate the experience, capture insights that arise during the practice, and solidify the connection between somatic awareness and emotional understanding.

- **Journaling:** Write down your thoughts and feelings.

Navigating the landscape of emotions through somatic therapy, these targeted exercises, practiced with intention and supplemented by complementary practices, offer a pathway to managing, understanding, and honoring our emotional states. Through the body's wisdom, we learn that every emotion, whether anxiety, sadness, or anger, carries the potential for growth, understanding, and ultimately transformation.

Building Resilience through Somatic Awareness

▢ Resilience

The ability to recover quickly from difficulties—emotional strength.

Resilience is a crucial aspect of human experience that helps individuals navigate life's transitions. In somatic therapy, resilience goes beyond its definition and involves a dynamic connection between physical and emotional well-being. This connection fosters an unbreakable spirit that can withstand adversity with grace and calmness.

Defining Resilience

Resilience is the capacity to recover swiftly from difficulties, a buoyancy of spirit that refuses to be submerged by the torrents of life's challenges. Its significance in somatic therapy is profound, offering a prism through which the healing journey can be viewed as an opportunity for growth and fortification. Resilience is not static but fluid, evolving through the body's engagement in practices that nurture strength, adaptability, and renewal. It is the silent roar of the ocean beneath the storm, powerful and serene, underscoring the inherent potential within to rise, time and again, with grace and strength.

Somatic Strategies for Resilience

Somatic therapy offers various techniques for building resilience and integrating it into an individual's physical and mental makeup. These strategies center around developing bodily awareness and attuning to somatic narratives that reveal untapped strength.

Consciously connecting with the earth through mindful movement, anchors the individual in the present and provides a stable foundation amid emotional upheaval.

- **Dynamic Grounding:**

  - Notice physical sensations of pressure, weight, and texture where your body touches the ground or any surface on which you're sitting or standing.

  - Take slow, deep breaths to center yourself and stay present.

  - Visualize roots extending from your feet into the earth, anchoring you securely.

  - Engage with your senses to anchor yourself in the present moment: notice the sights around you, listen closely to the sounds in your environment, pay attention to any scents in the air, and feel the textures of objects around you.

  - Incorporate gentle movements such as yoga, tai chi, or light stretching to release tension and promote embodiment.

  - Observe thoughts and emotions without judgment, returning focus to the present moment.

Another cornerstone practice that teaches the art of tension release is the symbolic shedding of the burdens that weigh heavily on both body and spirit. Progressive muscle relaxation is deliberate relaxation that fosters a sense of lightness and flexibility, qualities essential for resilience.

- **Progressive Muscle Relaxation:**

  - Find a quiet, comfortable space, and sit or lie in a relaxed position.

  - Close your eyes and bring your attention to your body.

  - Start with a specific muscle group, such as your hands or shoulders.

  - Inhale and tense the muscles in that group tightly, holding the tension for a few seconds.

- Exhale and suddenly release the tension in that muscle group, allowing it to relax completely.

- Notice the difference between tension and relaxation in the muscles.

- Move systematically through different muscle groups, from head to toe, progressively tensing and relaxing each one.

- Focus on your breath throughout the process, inhaling deeply as you tense the muscles and exhaling fully as you release the tension.

- Stay present and focused on the sensations in your body as you move through the relaxation sequence.

- Once you've relaxed all muscle groups, take a few moments to enjoy the overall sense of relaxation and calmness in your body.

Breathwork's profound simplicity acts as a potent catalyst for resilience. Techniques emphasizing deep, rhythmic breathing oxygenate the body, promoting physical well-being and synchronizing the body and mind, instilling a sense of calm and control. In moments of distress, the return to breath serves as a reminder of the individual's agency and ability to navigate the storm with breath as their compass.

- **Rhythmic Breathing:**

  - Find a comfortable seated or lying position in a quiet environment.

  - Close your eyes and pay attention to your breath.

  - Inhale slowly and deeply through your nose, counting to a comfortable rhythm, such as four counts.

  - Exhale slowly and completely through your mouth, matching the length of your exhale to your inhale, also counting to four.

- ○ Continue this rhythmic breathing pattern, inhaling and exhaling simultaneously, focusing on the smooth and steady rhythm of your breath.

- ○ Notice the sensation of your breath as it enters and leaves your body, feeling the rise and fall of your chest or abdomen.

- ○ Allow your body to relax with each breath, releasing tension and stress with each exhale.

- ○ Stay present and focused on the rhythm of your breath, letting go of any distracting thoughts or worries.

- ○ Practice rhythmic breathing for several minutes, gradually increasing the time as you become more comfortable with the technique.

- ○ When you're ready to finish, take a few deep breaths and slowly open your eyes, noticing how you feel after practicing rhythmic breathing.

Mindful movement integrates the body's wisdom with emotional fluidity, allowing for the expression and processing of emotions through physical narratives. Embodying emotion through movement fosters emotional resilience that complements its physical counterpart, creating a harmonious resilience that resonates through every aspect of being.

- • **Mindful Movements:** Practice yoga, tai chi, or spontaneous dance.

Integrating Resilience Practices

Seamlessly incorporating these resilience-building practices into the somatic routine necessitates an intuitive approach that honors the rhythms of the individual's life and the fluidity of their needs.

This integration begins with intention, the conscious decision to include resilience into the daily narrative, not as an added task but as a natural extension of existing routines. Selecting personally resonating practices ensures a more profound engagement, transforming them from exercises into rituals of strength and renewal.

Scheduling these practices during a period of relative calm allows individuals to build up a reserve of resilience that can be drawn upon in times of need. However, their true power is unlocked in times of adversity, guiding the individual back to the core of their strength.

Consistency is key, with regular engagement deepening the roots of resilience, allowing it to flourish and sustain the individual through life's inevitable storms.

Measuring Improvement

The path of resilience can be observed through personal and objective means, as it grows and strengthens over time.

Engage in self-reflection through practices like:

- **Journaling**

- **Meditation**

These can provide valuable insights into an individual's evolving ability to face adversity with groundedness and hopefulness.

Physical indicators such as:

- A decrease in stress-related symptoms.

- An enhanced capacity for relaxation.

They serve as tangible markers of the somatic aspect of resilience, reflecting the body's growing ability to recover and thrive in the face of stress.

Feedback from within the support network—therapists, peers, and loved ones—provides an external perspective on the individual's journey, highlighting shifts in demeanor, attitude, and engagement that may not be immediately apparent to the individual. This collective reflection, woven with personal insights, paints a comprehensive picture of resilience in growth, offering both validation of the journey thus far and inspiration for the path ahead.

This exploration of resilience within somatic therapy shifts the focus from coping with adversity to thriving amid it. Through targeted somatic strategies, intentional integration into daily life, and reflective improvement measures, individuals cultivate a deep and wide resilience that encompasses the physical, emotional, and spiritual.

This resilience, nurtured through conscious practice and engagement, is a testament to the human capacity for renewal and growth, embodying the essence of somatic therapy's transformative power.

Resourcing: Building a Foundation for Recovery

Resourcing in somatic therapy acts as a guiding principle that helps achieve grounded and expansive healing. Resourcing involves accessing internal and external anchors that foster a sense of safety, stability, and vitality. This foundational technique goes beyond simple coping methods, grounding individuals in a bedrock of support that enables them to face the highs and lows of emotional and bodily experiences with resilience and courage.

Resourcing is predicated on the understanding that everyone possesses innate strengths and external supports that, when consciously engaged, can significantly boost the process of healing and growth. These resources act as lighthouses, offering guidance and illumination through the stormy journey of recovery from trauma and stress. The brilliance of resourcing lies in its ability to be both a preparatory step and a continuous practice within somatic therapy, establishing an environment where individuals feel anchored enough to explore deeper emotional and somatic landscapes without becoming lost in them.

Identifying Resources

Identifying resources requires an introspective expedition—a deep dive into the sources of strength within and around us.

Personal resources encompass innate qualities such as:

- Resilience

- Humor

- Creativity

- A capacity for mindfulness

Techniques to uncover these treasures include:

- **Reflective Journaling:** Recount instances of overcoming adversity or moments of profound joy and connection.

- **Guided Visualization:** Visualize and embody your resources in a vivid, experiential manner which can facilitate a reconnection with your inner strengths.

Visualizations will be discussed further in Chapter 5.

Environmental resources include:

- Supportive relationships

- Serene natural settings

- Beloved pets

- Cherished objects that evoke a sense of comfort and peace

Mapping these external anchors involves an attentive observation of one's surroundings and interactions, noting the people, places, and things that consistently offer support and grounding. This seemingly simple mapping is a potent reminder of the network of support that surrounds each person, often going unnoticed in the rush of daily life.

Integrating Resources into Practice

Integrating identified resources into daily practice is both an art and a science, requiring creativity, intention, and regularity. It begins with the conscious decision to engage with these resources daily, whether through setting aside time for activities that reconnect one with one's inner strengths or ensuring regular contact with supportive individuals and environments.

Some daily resource ideas:

- Start your day by reading an inspirational quote that resonates with your resilience.

- Take a midday walk in a nearby park to immerse yourself in a nurturing natural environment.

- Carry a small object—a stone or a piece of jewelry—that serves as a tangible reminder of one's resources, offering comfort and connection when held during overwhelming moments.

- Spend time with your dog. They offer an unconditional presence, reminding you of the enduring support available in your immediate surroundings.

- Painting can be a wonderful outlet for expression and processing.

In moments of distress or facing challenging somatic exercises, one can actively call upon these resources to provide a grounding counterbalance. They can lift the spirit during difficult times, offering courage and stability. They highlight how, through intentional engagement with personal and environmental anchors, individuals can navigate the complexities of healing with a sense of safety and empowerment, transforming the recovery process into a journey of rediscovery and growth.

As we transition from exploring resourcing within somatic therapy, we recognize that healing is not a solitary endeavor. It's a combination of our internal strengths and the support that surrounds us. This acknowledgment, extending beyond the confines of therapy into the broader canvas of our lives, invites us to engage with ourselves and the world with a renewed sense of purpose and connection.

Utilizing Somatic Yoga for Emotional Release

Somatic yoga, a practice distinct from traditional forms, emphasizes the body's internal experiences and the release of stored emotions. This nuanced approach diverges from the pursuit of perfecting postures; instead, it delves into the sensations and emotional landscapes that each movement evokes. This modality fosters a deep dialogue with the body, encouraging practitioners to explore the spaces within which silence speaks volumes and movement becomes a healing narrative.

The essence of somatic yoga lies in its focus on the experiential, prioritizing the felt sense over the external form. In this practice, the body becomes a canvas; each pose is a stroke that reveals the underlying tensions and stories etched into the ligaments and fibers.

This method invites a gentle exploration of the body's boundaries and resistances, not to push through them but to understand and negotiate with them. It's a dialogue, a give-and-take, where movement and stillness converse in the language of sensation, creating an awareness that spans the scope of human experience.

In somatic yoga, specific poses and sequences are powerful tools for accessing and releasing emotional blockages.

Synchronized with breath, each movement peels away layers, revealing the emotional residues that cling to the body, inviting them into the light of conscious awareness for release and transformation.

Incorporating Mindfulness

Mindfulness, the art of present-moment awareness, intertwines seamlessly with somatic yoga, amplifying its impact on emotional healing. This integration transforms each posture into a moment of deep listening, a space where the body's whispers become audible. Individuals are encouraged to observe, without judgment, the sensations, emotions, and memories that arise with each movement. This mindful attention shifts the practice from a physical exercise to an emotional and somatic exploration, where the breath becomes a bridge between the seen and the unseen, between the known and the yet-to-be-discovered aspects of self.

Incorporating mindfulness into somatic yoga involves a conscious slowing down, an invitation to inhabit each pose fully, and the exploration of its landscapes with curiosity and openness. In this slowed pace, the body speaks, revealing its secrets in the tension released with a sigh, in the memories that surface with a stretch, in the emotions that flow with the breath. This mindful engagement with the body's language fosters a deep, compassionate connection with oneself, recognizing the body as a repository of lived experience deserving of care and attentiveness.

This is the part of the journey where movement and stillness become the mediums through which transformation is sought and found, where the body becomes a trusted ally in the quest for well-being, and where yoga becomes a dialogue with the deepest selves.

This link provides a 10-minute somatic yoga video to help release emotions – https://www.youtube.com/watch?v=WajHoXJac_c

SCAN ME

Chapter 4: Tools and Techniques

Managing Intense Emotions

- Grounding

- Pendulation

Self-Care Post Exercises

- Journaling

- Comforting physical activities

Exercises for Anxiety

- Earthing

- Herbal teas

Exercises for Sadness

- Fluid motion

- Create art

Exercises for Anger

- Dynamic release

- Engage in dialogue

Complimentary Exercises

- Mindfulness meditation

- Journaling

Strategies for Resilience

- Dynamic grounding

- Progressive muscle relaxation

- Rhythmic breathing

- Mindful movements

- Journaling

- Meditation

Identifying Resources

- Reflective journaling

- Guided visualization

Somatic Yoga for Emotional Release

- Somatic Yoga Video: https://www.youtube.com/watch?v=WajHo XJac_c

Request for a Review of "The Power of Somatic Therapy"

My goal is to make this valuable resource available to everyone, and you can help! Often, people pick books based on what others have said about them. By leaving your honest opinion of this book on Amazon, you can guide someone on their path to healing and self-discovery.

Your review can help someone:

- Recover from trauma; Cultivate self-compassion; Rediscover joy

- Strengthen relationships; Reduce panic attacks; Break free from limiting beliefs

I can't wait for you to discover the following chapters. We dive deeper into a holistic approach to trauma, coping with depression, addressing chronic pain, and so much more while providing powerful tools and exercises to guide you through those difficult times.

If you feel good about helping others, now is the perfect time to act.

Click here to leave your review on Amazon – https://www.amazon.com/review/review-your-purchases/?asin=B0D974BLTZ

SCAN ME

Thank you from the bottom of my heart for your support.

K. D. Anne

Chapter 5

Beyond the Basics

Visualization and Advanced Breathwork in Somatic Healing

The process of somatic healing is intertwined with our everyday experiences, subtly becoming a part of moments that are frequently ignored. It's in the way morning sunlight filters through the window, casting shadows that dance with the rhythm of our breath—a reminder of the world's continuous flow and our connection to it. Visualization, a cornerstone technique in somatic therapy, mirrors this interplay between light and shadow, guiding us to see beyond the surface of our physical experiences to the deeper stories held within our bodies. It's not a practice of escape but of deeper immersion in the here and now, enhancing presence and grounding individuals in their physical sensations with a clarity that goes beyond the ordinary.

The Role of Visualization in Somatic Healing

☐ Visualization

The practice of creating a mental image to promote relaxation, healing, or personal achievement.

Enhancing Presence

Visualization sharpens our awareness of the body's presence, like a photographer adjusts the lens to bring a scene into focus. Imagine standing in a forest; with each breath, the scent of pine fills your senses, the cool air brushes against your skin, and the sound of leaves rustling underfoot resonates. Even if this forest exists only in the mind, the body responds as though it were there, bridging gaps between the imagined and the real, enhancing bodily awareness and presence. This heightened state of awareness invites a more profound connection to our physical selves, directing attention inward from a quick glance to a steady focus.

Guided imagery serves as a conduit for healing, directing the mind toward visualizations that evoke physical and emotional responses conducive to healing. It's like listening to a piece of music that stirs emotions deep within, allowing for an emotional release without the need for words.

- **Guided Imagery:** Visualize a safe space where comfort, safety, and warmth embrace you, offering respite from stress or pain.

This mental imagery signals the body to relax, lowering heart rate and easing tension—a testament to the power of the mind-body connection.

Developing Custom Visualizations

Creating personalized visualizations demands an intimate knowledge of one's healing landscape. It begins with identifying scenarios, places, or experiences that inspire tranquility, strength, or joy. For some, it might be the memory of sitting by a gently flowing river; for others, it might be the feeling of sunlight warming their face. Translating these personal touchstones into vivid mental images involves engaging all the senses—sight, sound, touch, taste, and smell—to construct a multisensory experience that resonates on a deeply personal level.

- **Reflective Journaling:** Recount instances of overcoming adversity or moments of profound joy and connection.

This can aid in uncovering these touchstones, offering a space to explore and articulate the elements that contribute to a sense of well-being and groundedness.

Integrating Visualization with Movement

Pairing visualization with physical movement deepens the connection to somatic experiences, creating a dynamic interplay between the imagined and the tangible. Consider the practice of yoga; as one moves through the poses, visualizing energy flowing through the body can transform the practice from a series of physical movements into a deeply felt experience. Visualizing energy moving through tension or blockage areas enhances the poses' physical benefits. It engages the mind in a focused, meditative practice that unites body and spirit in a dance of healing and awareness.

This integration of visualization with movement can be adapted across various somatic practices, from mindful walking—where one visualizes absorbing the earth's energy with each step—to dance, where movements are infused with personal significance, each gesture a brushstroke in the painting of one's inner landscape.

Visualization is a practice of seeing not with the eyes but with the heart, engaging the body in a dialogue that transcends words, touching the core of our being. It's a reminder that healing and awareness begin with looking inward, guiding us to discover the landscapes within that await our exploration. Through the techniques of enhancing presence, using guided imagery for healing, developing custom visualizations, and integrating visualization with movement, we unlock the doors to a more profound somatic understanding, embarking on a path that leads to a reawakening of the senses—a rediscovery of the joy and wonder that reside in the simple act of being fully present in our bodies and in the world.

Advanced Breathwork Techniques for Deep Healing

Beyond the foundational practices of mindful inhalations and exhalations lies a realm where breath acts as a transformative force capable of unlocking profound layers of healing and emotional liberation. Advanced breathwork techniques, intricate in their design, offer a sophisticated approach to engaging with the body's innate wisdom, facilitating shifts that resonate at the core of one's being. These practices, steeped in ancient traditions yet refined for contemporary application, serve as a bridge to deeper realms of consciousness, unearthing hidden traumas and fostering an environment where true healing can flourish.

Exploring Advanced Breathwork Techniques

The intricate array of advanced breathwork techniques offers a diverse range of approaches, each method acting as a component that, when combined, creates a comprehensive approach to somatic healing.

Circular breathing is a continuous, unbroken flow of breath that blurs the lines between inhalation and exhalation, creating a loop of energy that courses through the body.

- **Circular Breathing:**

  - Inhale through the nose while storing air in the cheeks, then exhale through the mouth while simultaneously inhaling through the nose.

  - While exhaling through the mouth, inhale through the nose, enabling a seamless transition between inhalation and exhalation.

  - It requires practice to coordinate the alternating actions of storing air in the cheeks and inhaling through the nose.

This unending cycle fosters heightened awareness, where the usual boundaries of the self begin to dissolve, offering a glimpse into the interconnectedness of all things.

Holotropic breathwork invites participants on an inward odyssey, using rapid breathing to catalyze altered states of consciousness. This was developed by Dr. Stanislav Grof as a therapeutic approach to self-exploration and healing.

- **Holotropic Breathwork:**

  - Set an intention for your breathwork session, such as self-exploration, emotional healing, or spiritual growth.

○ Dim the lights, use candles or incense, and ensure comfort with blankets or cushions to create a supportive environment.

○ Lie down on your back or sit in a comfortable position with your eyes closed.

○ Begin breathing deeply and rhythmically, focusing on the inhalation and exhalation.

○ Use your breath to create a continuous, circular pattern, without pausing between inhales and exhales.

○ Allow your breath to become deeper and more intense as the session progresses, but avoid hyperventilating or forcing the breath.

○ Play music to enhance the experience, choosing tracks that resonate with your intentions.

○ Notice any physical sensations that arise as you breathe, such as tingling, warmth, or tension.

○ Allow yourself to surrender to the experience, trusting your body's innate wisdom to guide the process.

○ Be open to the possibility of emotional release, allowing suppressed feelings or memories to surface and be processed.

○ Welcome any emotions that arise with compassion and acceptance, knowing that they are part of the healing journey.

○ After the breathwork session, take time to reflect on your experience through journaling, artwork, or quiet contemplation.

In these expanded realms, insights surface, and emotional blockages, long barricaded, are gently eroded.

Physiological Impact

The effects of advanced breathwork on the body's physiology are profound and far-reaching. By manipulating the breath, one directly influences the autonomic nervous system, shifting from the sympathetic's fight-or-flight response to the parasympathetic's rest-and-digest state. This transition initiates a cascade of beneficial effects, including reduced blood pressure, decreased stress hormone levels, and enhanced immune function. The increased oxygenation of the blood and the subsequent release of endorphins during these practices contribute to a sense of euphoria and well-being, counteracting the lingering shadows of stress and trauma. Within this physiologically altered state, the body finds the space to initiate deep healing, repairing the wear of emotional scars and rebalancing the internal systems disrupted by past traumas.

Practicing Safely

While the benefits of advanced breathwork are undeniable, the journey into these profound practices necessitates caution, particularly for those with a history of trauma. For some, the intensity of the provoked experiences can trigger overwhelming emotional responses or reactivations of traumatic memories. Therefore, establishing a safe practice environment becomes paramount.

This begins with the guidance of a skilled facilitator, trained in the nuances of breathwork and adept at navigating the complexities of trauma-sensitive practice. Such a guide ensures that participants are fully informed of the potential experiences ahead, creating an atmosphere of trust and security. Participants are encouraged to remain in tune with their bodies throughout the process, honoring their limits and withdrawing from the practice if discomfort arises. The presence of grounding techniques, readily available to anchor participants back in the safety of the present moment, further enhances the practice's safety, ensuring that the journey into advanced breathwork remains a path of healing rather than harm.

Shared Experiences

During my journey, I participated in group breathwork sessions. Some intense emotions surfaced within the group, and many chose to share their experiences.

One woman shared that she was trapped by chronic anxiety. She was skeptical about entering the practice but found liberation through circular breathing. She described a profound inner peace that had been unattainable for a long time. The continuous cycle of breath became a rhythmic anchor, offering not just moments of respite but a sustained shift toward tranquility.

Another person was confronted with unresolved grief. Holotropic breathwork served as their vessel, guiding them through turbulent emotional waters to a place of acceptance and release. The rapid breathing drove them into a state of heightened emotional receptivity, where memories, long buried, surfaced as teachers. Through this journey, they encountered their grief as a part of their story to be acknowledged and integrated, paving the way for a newfound sense of wholeness.

For myself, I've learned to use breathwork to offer me clarity. When life seems overwhelming, and my thoughts spiral out of control, I can tap into my breath quickly, saving me from the undesirable path I was headed on. Darkness suddenly turns into sunlight.

The potential within the breath holds the power to heal, liberate, and renew.

Chapter 5: Tools and Techniques

Visualization

- Guided imagery

- Reflective journaling

Advanced Breathwork Techniques

- Circular breathing

- Holotropic breathwork

Chapter 6

Trauma and Transformation

Somatic Strategies for Recovery and Reconnection

We touched on trauma briefly in Chapter 1. Since it affects and disrupts the lives of millions of people worldwide, I'd like to delve a little deeper into the subject.

Trauma's Impact on the Body

Our bodies carry the echoes of trauma within their very being long before the mind can even begin to comprehend and unravel the pain. Infiltrating the body's systems, trauma disrupts the harmonious dialogue between flesh and spirit, embedding itself in the muscle's memory, the nervous system's wiring, and the heart's rhythm. This disruption manifests as a physical discomfort and a profound disconnection from one's bodily existence. The body, which once felt like an ally, becomes a stranger, its signals of distress and discomfort a foreign language that baffles and overwhelms. Addressing trauma, therefore, demands a somatic approach, one that acknowledges the body not just as a site of pain but as a key participant in the healing process. It requires a relearning of the body's language, a patient unraveling of the stories it holds, and a gentle reintegration of mind and body toward a state of holistic well-being.

Fight, Flight, Freeze Responses

In the face of threat, the body's primal instincts are activated, steering one toward survival through the innate responses of fight, flight, or freeze. While crucial in acute danger, these responses often become dysfunctionally imprinted into the body's repertoire, activated long after the threat has passed. The body, caught in the grip of these responses, relives the trauma in a loop of heightened alertness, hyperarousal, or numbing immobility. Muscles may remain tense for battle, breaths shallow in anticipation of flight, or limbs immobilized in a freeze response that mutes the world's chaos. The somatic implications are profound, as these hyperarousal or hypoarousal states disrupt the body's natural equilibrium, leading to a cascade of physical and emotional disturbances that shadow one's existence.

Somatic Symptoms of Trauma

Trauma inscribes itself on the body in a catalog of symptoms that whisper of distress long after the mind has sought to bury the memories. These symptoms, often dismissed or misattributed to unrelated physical ailments, serve as the body's testimony to its unprocessed suffering. Chronic pain without clear medical origin, inexplicable fatigue that drapes the body in lethargy, digestive disturbances that defy dietary explanation, and hypersensitivity to sensory stimuli that once felt harmless—these are only a few of the somatic echoes of trauma. Recognizing these symptoms as the body's language of distress requires a nuanced understanding, an attunement to the subtle ways the body communicates its pain and its need for healing.

Holistic Approach to Trauma

Somatic therapy, with its emphasis on the embodied experience, offers a holistic approach to understanding and addressing trauma, one that honors the body as a vast repository of wisdom and a pathway to recovery.

This approach begins with the following:

- **Somatic Mindfulness:** Listen deeply to the body's signals, acknowledging each sensation, however faint or overwhelming, as a guide toward healing.

Somatic tracking involves gently observing the shifting landscapes of bodily sensations. It fosters a reconnection with the body and transforms the experience of somatic symptoms from one of alienation to one of understanding.

- **Somatic Tracking:**

  - Begin by noticing and acknowledging all bodily sensations, whether pain-related or not.

  - Observe the sensations without attempting to change them. Focus on describing the sensations rather than evaluating them.

  - Understand that sensations, including pain, are normal body signals and not necessarily indicators of harm.

  - Imagine pain as a neutral object that can be modified (in size, color, or intensity) through mental imagery. This helps us conceptualize pain as something controllable.

  - Encourage a calm and nonreactive response to sensations, fostering a sense of safety and control.

Movement encourages the body to express what words cannot and move through patterns of freeze and immobility toward fluidity and strength.

- **Guided Movement Practices:**

  - Start with deep, slow breaths to calm the nervous system.

  - Introduce simple, flowing movements that are repetitive and soothing, such as:

    - Gentle rolling of the neck and shoulders.

    - Raising the arms slowly overhead and lowering them.

    - Swaying side to side.

    - Gentle twisting of the torso from side to side.

Therapeutic touch rekindles the sense of safety within the body, soothing the hyperarousal of the fight or flight responses and awakening sensations numbed by the freeze response.

- **Therapeutic Touch:** Administer with consent and attunement to the individual's boundaries.

In this holistic paradigm, movement and touch emerge as powerful modalities for re-engaging with the body, offering avenues for releasing stored trauma and restoring bodily autonomy.

This comprehensive approach to trauma recognizes the intricate interplay between body and psyche, between the physiological imprints of trauma and the emotional narratives that accompany them. It acknowledges that healing from trauma is not a linear progression but a spiral journey that revisits old wounds with new insights, gradually fostering resilience and renewal.

Through the practices of somatic therapy, individuals are invited to reclaim their bodies from the shadows of trauma, to reforge the broken connection between flesh and spirit, and to embark on a path that leads not back to the person they were before the trauma but forward to the person they are becoming in its aftermath.

Somatic Grounding Techniques for Trauma Triggers

In the aftermath of trauma, the world may not resemble the sanctuary it once was; spaces once filled with warmth can suddenly echo with the coldness of past fears, and moments of solitude might morph into unwelcome gateways to memories best left untouched.

Within this altered landscape, the body does not forget—it stores, it recalls, and in moments least expected, it reacts, manifesting trauma triggers that ripple through the fabric of existence with unsettling ease.

Navigating this terrain requires more than will; it demands a return to the body, not as a site of distress but as a ground of healing and safety.

Somatic grounding techniques emerge as vital practices in this reclamation, offering strategies specifically tailored to anchor the self in the face of trauma triggers to transform the body from a vessel of vulnerability to one of resilience and peace.

Grounding for Trauma Triggers

Trauma triggers—those unexpected jolts that transport one back to moments of fear, helplessness, or pain—demand a response that not only addresses the immediate surge of emotion but also re-establishes a sense of control and safety. Somatic grounding techniques provide such a response, engaging the body's senses to tether the mind to the present, to the tangible, the real, and the now.

Tactile grounding acts as a lifeline, pulling one back from the precipice of past traumas.

- **Tactile Grounding:** Focus intently on the sensations of an object—a stone's cool smoothness, the fabric's weave under fingertips.

The following technique is a timekeeper of safety. Each beat reminds the body of its presence in a safe here and now, away from the shadows of the past.

- **Rhythmic Movement:** Use simple swaying or foot tapping.

Personalized Grounding Strategies

The personalization of grounding strategies acknowledges each individual's experience with trauma, understanding that what anchors one may not serve another. This customization involves an intimate dialogue with oneself, a questioning that probes into the nature of one's triggers and the inner landscapes that provide comfort.

To anchor the self firmly in the present use visualization and auditory grounding.

- **Visualization:** Imagine roots extending from the soles, delving deep into the earth's core, and drawing strength and stability.

- **Auditory Grounding:** Focus on a symphony of everyday sounds—a clock's ticking, a bird's song, the rhythmic inhale and exhale of breath.

Always working within a safe space, experimentation and reflection guide this process, crafting a suite of personalized strategies that not only ground but resonate with profound significance.

Through these practices, individuals learn to anchor themselves in the safety of the now, transforming their relationship with their bodies, memories, and, ultimately, their selves.

Somatic Experiencing: Moving through Trauma

Somatic experiencing, rooted in the understanding that trauma resides not just in the mind but also in the body, proposes a path forward that is both gentle and profound. It rests on the foundational belief that the body possesses an inherent ability to heal itself, a concept that, while ancient in its wisdom, finds new life in the practices of somatic experiencing. This approach does not seek to dredge up trauma for trauma's sake but to engage with it in a way that enables the body to process and release it, fostering a return to balance and wholeness.

Principles of Somatic Experiencing

At the heart of somatic experiencing lies a trio of principles guiding its practice: titration, pendulation, and creating a felt sense.

- **Titration:** Focus on breaking down overwhelming experiences into manageable pieces, allowing yourself to engage with your trauma without becoming re-traumatized.

- **Pendulation:** Focus on moving between states of trauma activation and states of safety or neutrality, fostering the body's natural rhythm of arousal and rest.

- **Creating a Felt Sense:**

  - Access and experience bodily sensations and feelings associated with past experiences or current emotions.

  - Tune into the body's physical sensations, such as tension, warmth, or tightness.

  - Allow those sensations to guide the exploration of underlying emotions and memories.

The cornerstone of this process is having a deep, bodily understanding of one's experiences. This bridges the cognitive understanding of trauma and its somatic resolution.

Together, these principles enable individuals to touch upon their traumatic memories in a controlled manner, facilitating healing without overwhelming the nervous system.

Somatic Experiencing Techniques

The techniques employed in somatic experiencing are as varied as those seeking its healing touch.

The following practice fosters an awareness of the body's signals, often revealing tension, heaviness, or constriction patterns directly linked to traumatic experiences.

- **Tracking Bodily Sensations:** Notice and describe the physical manifestations of your emotions and memories.

Resourcing will help provide a stable ground to engage with difficult memories.

- **Resourcing:** Focus on identifying and drawing upon internal and external sources of strength and comfort. (See Chapter 4)

Through these and other techniques, somatic experiencing gently guides individuals toward the reintegration of mind and body, transforming the experience of trauma from one of disconnection and disempowerment to one of understanding and control.

Trauma Processing

Unlike approaches that rely solely on verbal recounting of traumatic events, somatic experiencing engages the body as an active participant in the healing process. It recognizes that trauma often renders its victims speechless, trapped in a body that has become a source of fear and betrayal. Through somatic experiencing, individuals learn to listen to their bodies and decode the language of sensations and movements that speak volumes where words fail. This bodily engagement allows for the processing of trauma as an experience to be felt and ultimately released. It is a process that unfolds slowly, with respect for the individual's pace and boundaries, always prioritizing safety and the restoration of a sense of control and empowerment.

Through the principles and techniques of somatic experiencing, individuals find a path that honors their experiences, engages their bodies in the healing process, and, ultimately, leads them toward restoring wholeness and vitality.

Shared Experiences

A close friend of mine shared with me her journey of overcoming the aftermath of a violent assault. Although she wishes to keep her identity anonymous, I am honored to share that she found solace in somatic experiencing. This approach allowed her to confront her trauma without feeling overwhelmed by it. Through the practice of tracking bodily sensations, she began to recognize the physical patterns that self-regulation accompanied her flashbacks and anxiety—a tightness in her chest, and a quickening of her breath. Gradually, with guidance and support, she learned to navigate these sensations, employing grounding techniques that brought her back to a state of safety. Over time, the intensity of her flashbacks diminished, replaced by a growing sense of control over her reactions and a newfound trust in her body's capacity to heal.

Denis, the veteran I mentioned previously, was plagued by nightmares and hypervigilance, hallmarks of post-traumatic stress disorder. Somatic experiencing offered him a way to explore the somatic roots of his hyperarousal, identifying the bodily sensations that preceded his episodes of panic and aggression. Through pendulation, he discovered a rhythm to his trauma responses, learning to oscillate between activation and relaxation. This awareness, coupled with resourcing techniques that drew upon his love for nature and music, provided him with the tools to calm his nervous system, reducing the frequency and severity of his symptoms. His journey through somatic experiencing brought not just relief from his suffering but a profound shift in his relationship with his body, from a source of torment to a wellspring of healing and peace.

Pendulation: Finding Balance within the Body

The Concept of Pendulation

Within the complex journey of healing, particularly from trauma, the body often finds itself oscillating between states of comfort and discomfort, a phenomenon at the heart of pendulation. This concept, deeply rooted in somatic experiencing, is a method that can gently navigate traumatic memories, exploring the terrain between dysregulation—where the body's responses might feel overwhelming or disconnected—and regulation, a state of balance and stability. Pendulation, in essence, respects the body's innate wisdom, acknowledging its capacity to move toward healing when given the space to explore its rhythm of activation and settling. Through this oscillation, the individual gradually cultivates a deeper sense of safety within their body, fostering an environment where healing is possible and facilitated in a gentle way.

Pendulation Techniques

Pendulation leverages techniques that invite the body to express and process traumatic energy without becoming trapped.

- **Attentive Observation:** Identify bodily sensations where trauma manifests as tension or numbness.

- **Shifting Your Focus:** Focus between sensations of tension or numbness and areas of neutrality or pleasant sensations, initiating the pendulation process.

Moving attention, like a pendulum's swing, allows for a gradual desensitization to traumatic stimuli, easing the body's grip on past pains.

Through repeated practice, this technique mitigates the intensity of traumatic responses and enhances the body's capacity to self-regulate, laying down new pathways of resilience and recovery.

Building Resilience

The journey through pendulation, with its gentle oscillations between states of ease and challenge, naturally fosters resilience within the nervous system. This resilience emerges not from avoiding difficult sensations or memories but from intentional engagement with these experiences in a controlled and supportive manner.

Each swing of the pendulum strengthens the nervous system's ability to tolerate stress and return to a state of balance, much like a muscle grows through the stress and release of exercise. Over time, this process builds a robust foundation, enabling the individual to face life's adversities with renewed confidence and stability.

The body, once a battleground of traumatic reenactments, transforms into a sanctuary of strength and adaptability, capable of navigating both internal and external stressors with a composed grace.

Practical Exercises

Incorporate pendulation into your daily practices.

- **Pendulation:**

  - Begin with an anchor—a physical or mental point of safety that serves as a home base throughout the exercise. This anchor could be a comforting memory, a soothing sensation, or even a supportive object.

  - Turn your attention to a sensation associated with discomfort or distress, perhaps a tightness in the chest or heaviness in the shoulders, and allow yourself to fully feel this sensation for a moment.

  - Redirect your attention to the anchor, the sensation or memory of safety and comfort.

  - Repeat this oscillation, spending more time exploring the edges of discomfort in each cycle and always returning to the anchor as a regrounding.

As navigation tools:

- **Incorporate Breath:** Use inhalations to explore challenging sensations and exhalations to return to the anchor.

- **Use Imagery:** Visualize the movement between states of activation and calm as a journey through different landscapes, each with its own textures, colors, and emotions.

When engaged with regularity and intention, these practical exercises demystify the body's traumatic responses and celebrate its capacity for healing and balance.

Through pendulation, individuals learn to ride the waves of their experiences with an assured poise, moving through life's challenges with a resilience born from the body's deep wells of wisdom and strength.

Pendulation, thus, stands as a testament to the body's remarkable ability to navigate the complexities of healing from trauma. It underscores a profound truth at the heart of somatic therapy—that within the body lie the echoes of past pains and the keys to liberation and wholeness. Through the rhythmic dance of pendulation, individuals reclaim their bodies as allies in the journey toward healing, discovering along the way a balance and resilience that radiate beyond the confines of therapy into the full spectrum of their lives.

Titration: Managing the Intensity

Mainly from the invisible wounds of trauma, there exists a delicate balance between confronting pain and nurturing safety. Within this balance, titration emerges as a critical process like slowly dripping a substance into another, achieving a controlled and transformative reaction. This concept, borrowed from chemistry, finds profound application in somatic experiencing, offering a systematic approach to navigating the often turbulent waters of traumatic memories. By breaking down overwhelming experiences into digestible segments, titration permits individuals to process trauma without the risk of retraumatization, fostering an environment where healing can unfold with measured grace.

Titration embodies a philosophy of care that prioritizes the individual's capacity for processing distress. It recognizes the inherent danger in unearthing trauma too quickly or too fully, which can overwhelm the nervous system, leaving individuals in a state of heightened vulnerability. Titration serves as a safeguard, a method that ensures the pacing of therapeutic exploration aligns with the individual's ability to integrate and heal.

In practice, this might involve:

- Focusing on a fragment of a memory rather than its entirety.

- Exploring the physical sensations associated with a traumatic event instead of its emotional content.

This allows the individual to remain anchored in the present, feeling stable in their surroundings, even as they venture into the painful territories of their past.

The empowerment of individuals to apply titration techniques independently marks a significant evolution in the healing journey. Accessible and adaptable self-titration tools equip individuals with the means to navigate their healing process with autonomy and insight.

A "Somatic Thermometer" is a mental gauge that monitors the intensity of bodily sensations, emotions, or memories. This self-monitoring fosters a deepened awareness of one's thresholds and capacities, encouraging a proactive approach to managing distress.

- **The "Somatic Thermometer":**

  - Assign a numerical value to your current level of discomfort or activation.

  - Decide whether to proceed with your exploration or to step back and employ grounding techniques.

Breathing exercises serve as potent instruments for self-titration. This control over one's physiological responses not only mitigates the impact of distressing memories or sensations but also reinforces a sense of control, a pivotal element in the landscape of trauma recovery. Individuals can directly influence their nervous system, dialing down the intensity of activation and facilitating a return to a state of balance.

- **Breathing Exercise**: Modulate the breath—elongating exhalations to extend beyond inhalations.

The benefits of titration extend far into long-term healing, laying a foundation for resilience and wholeness to flourish. By calibrating the exposure to traumatic material to the individual's capacity for integration, titration cultivates a sense of safety that envelops the therapeutic process. This safety, consistently reinforced, becomes internalized, transforming the individual's relationship with their trauma. No longer does the past hold the power to hijack the present with unexpected intensity; instead, memories and emotions can be engaged with mindfulness and intention. This subtle yet profound shift marks a pivotal turn in the journey of healing, where individuals can encounter their traumas as facets of their experience that, though painful, can be navigated with grace and resilience.

This transformation is about evolving in the aftermath of trauma and moving toward a future where the scars of the past no longer restrict the fullness of one's existence.

Dynamic Movement to Reconnect with the Body

Dynamic movement principles are the foundation for reconnecting with one's body and emotions. This method acknowledges the body as a living archive of experiences, where each muscle twitch and posture shift is a narrative waiting to be explored. The principles advocate for an intuitive approach to movement, encouraging individuals to let go of preconceived notions of structure and form, allowing the body to guide the exploration. In this freeform expression, the body finds space to communicate its untold stories, using movement as a language to express what words cannot.

Understanding movement as a language of the body that conveys emotions and experiences requires a shift in perspective. It asks for deep listening, an attunement to the subtle whispers and shouts that our physical form articulates. This language is not universal; it is deeply personal, shaped by the contours of individual experiences and the shadows they cast. It speaks of the tension held in shoulders, the curve of a spine retreating inwards, the exuberant leap of joy, and the grounded stance of resilience. To engage with this language is to engage in a dialogue with the self, a conversation that bridges the gap between the seen and the unseen, the known and the mysterious depths of our being.

Creating personal movement routines that resonate with individual needs begins with this understanding. It involves experimentation, trying different forms of movement as one would outfits, and observing which ones fit the contours of their current emotional and physical state.

A range of routines:

- Structured dance

- Exploratory free movement in a safe space

- Vigorous physical exercise

- Gentle stretches that honor the body's need for rest

The key is in the intention—the conscious decision to use movement as a tool for self-exploration and healing.

Guidelines for creating these routines emphasize the importance of flexibility, encouraging individuals to adapt their practices as their bodies and emotional landscapes shift. It is a dynamic process that evolves along the individual's journey, reflecting their growth, challenges, and discoveries.

The role of the community in dynamic movement practices can be beneficial. Shared movement experiences foster a profound sense of connection, a recognition of the universality of our struggles and triumphs. In a group setting, whether in a dance class, a yoga session, or a therapeutic movement workshop, individuals find their experiences mirrored in others, a powerful reminder of our shared humanity. This communal aspect of dynamic movement adds a layer of richness to the practice, transforming it from a solitary exploration to a collective journey. It nurtures a sense of belonging, offering support and validation that enhances individuals' efforts to reconnect with their bodies and emotions. The energy of a group moving in unison—each person engaged in their dialogue with the self yet connected by the rhythm of shared movement—creates a palpable force. This healing energy transcends the boundaries of personal experience.

In exploring dynamic movement to reconnect with the body, we discover a path that leads us back to ourselves. It is a path paved with the understanding that movement is a language through which our bodies speak, a method to unravel the narratives woven into our muscles and bones. Through creating personal movement routines guided by the principles of dynamic movement and nurtured within the embrace of community, we find a way to listen, respond, and heal. This journey through movement becomes a dance of discovery, where each step, each gesture, and each pause is an act of reconnection, a step toward wholeness.

As we conclude this exploration of dynamic movement, it becomes evident that the journey to reconnect with our bodies is both deeply personal and profoundly universal. The journey honors the body's capacity to hold and heal from our experiences, employing movement to unlock the emotions and stories etched within our physical form. In doing so, we not only rediscover the language of our bodies but also learn to speak it with fluency and grace, fostering a connection that resonates with the rhythms of healing and growth. This process, reflective of the broader themes of somatic therapy, invites us into a deeper engagement with ourselves and the world around us, preparing us for the continued exploration of the transformative power of somatic practices.

Chapter 6: Tools and Techniques

Holistic Approach to Trauma

- Somatic mindfulness

- Somatic tracking

- Guided movement practices

- Therapeutic touch

Grounding for Trauma Triggers

- Tactile grounding

- Rhythmic movement

- Visualization

- Auditory grounding

Somatic Experiencing – Moving through Trauma

- Tracking bodily sensations

- Resourcing

Pendulation – Finding Balance within the Body

- Attentive observation

- Shifting your focus

- Incorporate breath

- Use imagery

Tools for Titration – Managing Intensity

- A somatic thermometer

- Breathing exercise

Reconnect with the Body

- Dynamic movement

Chapter 7

Restoring Balance

Somatic Techniques for Stress, Pain, and Emotional Wellness

"The power that made the body can heal the body." – BJ Palmer

In our modern lives, stress has become so tightly woven into our daily existence that we often fail to notice it until it starts to pull at the seams. It's like a constant background noise in a cafe that we are so used to that we don't even realize it's there until it stops. This chapter aims to unravel the patterns of stress that have become part of our daily lives and provide somatic tools that can help manage and transform our relationship with stress.

Somatic Tools for Stress Management

The body, a repository of stress, holds tension like a book retains ink, each muscle contraction a word, each shallow breath a sentence in the narrative of our daily struggles. Somatic therapy offers techniques to rewrite this narrative, turning pages filled with tension into chapters of relief.

Progressive muscle relaxation teaches the body the contrast between stress and relaxation. It's like the relief felt when, after holding a heavy suitcase for a long time, it's finally set down; the arms still hum with the memory of the weight, but the relief is palpable.

- **Progressive Muscle Relaxation:** Apply tension to different muscle groups and then release it. (Explained in detail in Chapter 4.)

Integrating this practice into daily routines offers a way to manage stress continuously. It could be as simple as setting reminders to check in with one's posture and breathing throughout the day, like watering plants at intervals to ensure they thrive. This regular attention to bodily sensations becomes a thread of mindfulness that weaves through the fabric of our day, preventing stress from embedding itself too profoundly.

Understanding the stress response is crucial for effective management. When we perceive a threat, the body's fight or flight response is triggered, releasing cortisol and adrenaline, and preparing the body for action. Recognizing this response for what it is—an ancient survival mechanism ill-suited to modern stressors—allows us to engage with it differently. Instead of becoming over-whelmed by the body's response to stress, we can observe it with curiosity, employing somatic techniques like deep, diaphragmatic breathing to signal the brain that the perceived threat has passed, slowing the heart rate and calming the nervous system.

Daily Practices

The morning offers a blank canvas, a moment ripe with potential before the day's stresses begin to paint their strokes.

Starting the day with a somatic grounding exercise can anchor us, offering stability in the face of the day's uncertainties.

- **Earthing:** Stand barefoot on the earth, feeling the cool grass or the rough texture of concrete. Take deep breaths, visualizing roots growing from our feet deep into the ground.

This connection to the earth reminds us of the present moment, counterbal-ancing the mind's tendency to dwell on past worries or future anxieties.

Late afternoon, when the day's demands often peak, presents an opportunity for a brief somatic pause. Focused stretching can act like a reset button, releasing tension and refreshing the mind.

- **Focused Stretching:** Target areas where you typically hold stress—shoulders, neck, lower back.

As the day winds down, a reflective somatic practice helps process the day's stresses.

- **Body Scanning:** Lie down and mentally traverse the body from head to toe, noting areas of tension or ease and acknowledging them without judgment.

This practice is like sifting through the day's mail and sorting junk from what truly needs attention. It allows us to release unnecessary tension and retain only what serves us.

Techniques for Easing Anxiety and Panic Attacks

Anxiety can be a fierce obstacle to overcome when dealing with human emotions. It can cause sudden panic attacks and disrupt our daily life. Navigating through these turbulent times takes more than just willpower. We must develop a map and compass of techniques and understanding to provide immediate and long-lasting relief. By cultivating these navigational tools, we can create a safe environment where panic is no longer a constant threat.

Immediate Relief Techniques

At the onset of an anxiety attack, the body becomes a battleground where the breath turns shallow, the heart races, and the world seems to contract. In these moments, grounding techniques act as anchors, drawing the self back from the precipice of panic.

The following method engages all five senses to halt the spiral of anxiety. It brings the mind back to the tangible world, diluting the potency of panic.

- **The 5-4-3-2-1 Method:** Name five (5) things one can see, four (4) things one can touch, three (3) things one can hear, two (2) things one can smell, and one (1) thing one can taste.

The act of mental compartmentalization allows for a temporary distancing from anxiety, providing space to breathe and recalibrate. When wielded with intention, visualization becomes a tool of mastery over the moment, offering a pause in the relentless narrative of panic.

- **The Practice of Containment:** Visualize and place distressing thoughts or overwhelming emotions into an imaginary box.

Long-Term Strategies

The foundation of long-term resilience against anxiety is built upon routine somatic awareness.

A practice as simple yet profound as daily journaling cultivates an attunement to the early whispers of anxiety, allowing for intervention before whispers become roars. Over time, this journal becomes a map of one's somatic landscape, revealing patterns and triggers of anxiety that were once veiled in the chaos of the mind.

- **Journal Daily:** Write down your bodily sensations.

- **Incorporate Regular Somatic Exercises:** Practice yoga or qi gong daily.

These act as preventative measures and create a peaceful environment that is strong enough to withstand sudden panic attacks.

By prioritizing breath and movement, these techniques promote a state of balance between the body and mind, which reduces the disharmony that often gives rise to anxiety. Over time, the body learns a new rhythm, one where the echoes of past panic attacks grow fainter, replaced by a steadier pulse of tranquility.

Understanding Triggers

To overcome anxiety, it is important to identify the triggers that cause it.

This can be done by:

- Mapping out the situations or events that lead to panic.

It may seem overwhelming, but it is a necessary step toward disarming anxiety. By reflecting on past experiences, you can uncover hidden triggers that may seem insignificant, such as:

- A particular smell

- Time of day

- Type of music

Once these triggers are identified, you can avoid them or work on desensitizing yourself to them.

It is equally essential to:

- Recognize internal triggers that can stem from our thoughts and beliefs.

- Identify and challenge distorted or negative thought patterns that contribute to emotional distress.

- Replace irrational or unhelpful thoughts with more realistic and adaptive ones.

We can reframe anxious thoughts and transform them into messages of insight. This can help us challenge their power and ground ourselves in the present reality. By doing so, we can reclaim control over our internal landscape and reduce the impact of triggers on our lives.

Lifestyle adjustments also play a crucial role in this endeavor.

To reduce the overall volume of anxiety's chatter incorporate:

- **Mindfulness**

- **Regular physical activity**

- **Nutritional balance**

In crafting these techniques and strategies, the individual becomes both a cartographer and navigator of their journey through anxiety, charting a course that leads where anxiety no longer reigns with unchecked power. It is a journey marked not by the absence of storms but by the skill to weather them, a voyage where each technique is mastered and each strategy is implemented to serve as a beacon, guiding the way toward calmer seas.

Coping with Depression through Somatics

Depression can be an overwhelming experience that drains the colors of life and makes every day feel like a dreary, gray landscape. When we're in the grips of depression, our body can become both a battlefield and a sanctuary. That's where somatic therapy comes in. Exercises designed to counteract the effects of depression can be incredibly effective when grounded in this wisdom. By reconnecting to our body's innate capacity for joy and resilience, we can find some relief from the heavy weight of depression.

The dialogue between mind and body, often silenced by depression, finds its voice again through somatic practices. This re-established communication reveals how depression colors perception, how it tightens muscles in a physical manifestation of emotional pain, and how it disrupts the breath, the life force that sustains us. Somatic exercises encourage listening and attentiveness to these subtle cues. They teach the language of the body, allowing for a conversation that moves beyond words, reaching into the heart of emotional distress to soothe and heal.

This connection illuminates the pathway from depression to well-being, highlighting how somatic awareness can shift mood, lift the fog of lethargy, and ignite the spark of vitality dimmed by depression. It is a testament to the body's resilience and capacity to carry us through the darkest times and emerge into light.

Routines play an important role in our daily lives by providing structure and predictability amid the chaos. By integrating somatic exercises into these routines, we can add a layer of intentionality and self-care to our daily lives, which can help counter the feelings of despair that often accompany depression. This way, we can create a positive pattern that promotes well-being and mental health.

Somatic Exercises for Depression

Mindful movement, such as that found in somatic yoga, encourages the flow of energy and the release of physical and emotional stagnation.

- **Mindful Movements:** Practice yoga or qi gong.

This link provides a video to help cope with depression: https://www.youtube.com/watch?v=Sxddnugwu-8

SCAN ME

Imagine the body as a river: depression, the dam that halts its flow. Somatic exercises gently dismantle this barrier, allowing turbulent and calm emotions to move freely. Setting aside time each morning to engage in mindful movement sets the tone for the day—a declaration of self-compassion and a step toward healing.

Breathwork is a powerful tool for individuals to anchor themselves in the present, a counterpoint to depression, which anchors in the past's regrets or the future's anxieties.

- **Breathwork:** Focus on the rhythm of the breath drawing in vitality with each inhalation and releasing the weight of sorrow with each exhalation.

The harmony between activity and rest, giving and receiving, holding on, and letting go, balanced with periods of relaxation, mirrors the balance sought in life.

- **Stretching:** Target areas where you typically hold stress—shoulders, neck, lower back.

Evening practices, whether through breathwork or stretching, offer a moment to release the day's accumulated stress, preparing the ground for restorative sleep.

This dynamic balance fosters an environment where depression's grip loosens and where the body and mind can find a meeting point in healing. This routine becomes a sanctuary, a space carved out of time for self-connection and healing.

By repeating somatic practices, wellness habits take root, slowly but surely transforming the landscape of depression into one of hope and vitality.

Community Support

The power of the shared community practice in the journey through depression is crucial. Individuals find guidance and solidarity in spaces where somatic exercises are practiced together, whether in classes, workshops, or informal gatherings. The energy of a group engaged in collective healing amplifies the effects of somatic practices, creating a resonance that vibrates through each participant, reminding them they are not alone in their struggle.

These communities serve as mirrors, reflecting the possibility of joy and the capacity for resilience that depression often obscures. They offer support beyond the sessions, a network of connections that sustains individuals in moments of doubt and isolation. In this shared space, stories of struggle and triumph mingle, weaving a narrative of collective resilience that protects against depression's isolating force.

The path through depression, marked by somatic exercises, is one of reconnection—to the body, to the present moment, and to the community. It is a journey that honors the depth of despair and the potential for renewal, acknowledging the darkness but moving steadily toward the light. In this movement, in this intention to heal, lies the power to transform the experience of depression, to find within it the seeds of growth and the promise of a brighter tomorrow.

Addressing Chronic Pain with Somatic Methods

For those whose lives are impacted by chronic pain, somatic therapy shines as a light of hope, offering relief and insight. This method is based on the body's innate intelligence. It aims not only to alleviate symptoms but also to communicate with pain, understand its messages, and employ techniques that target its causes and effects.

Somatic Techniques for Pain

The landscape of somatic therapy is rich with techniques designed to ease the burden of chronic pain. Through slow, intentional movements, individuals learn to explore the edges of their pain, to move with and through it rather than in opposition.

- **Mindful Movements:** Practice yoga or qi gong.

They stand out for their ability to gently coax the body away from patterns of tension and contraction that exacerbate pain. This gentle exploration shifts the body's relationship with pain from struggle to coexistence, where moments of ease become possible and even frequent.

This link provides a video to help address chronic pain: https://www.yout ube.com/watch?v=62k71bFeyOA

SCAN ME

Breathwork, another cornerstone of somatic therapy, offers a direct route to the nervous system, which plays a pivotal role in the experience of pain.

- **Diaphragmatic Breathing:** Focus on the rise and fall of your belly during each inhalation and exhalation.

This activates the parasympathetic nervous system, signaling the body to relax and unwind. This relaxation response can mitigate pain's intensity, offering moments of respite that can gradually extend into periods of sustained relief.

When integrated into daily life, breathwork becomes a tool for managing pain, a method of interrupting the cycle of stress and tension that so often accompanies chronic pain conditions.

Understanding Pain Signals

To engage effectively with pain, one must first understand its language, signals, and what it signifies about the body's needs and conditions.

Pain, in its essence, is a message, an alert that something within requires attention. Somatic therapy encourages a curious and nonjudgmental approach to these signals, inviting individuals to explore their pain with openness and compassion.

This exploration involves a passive reception of pain's messages and an active engagement, asking, "What does this pain mean?" and "How can I respond in a way that brings relief and healing?"

This understanding of pain signals transforms the experience of chronic pain from one of helpless endurance to one of empowered action. It shifts the locus of control back to the individual, who, armed with knowledge and techniques, can engage with their pain in a proactive and healing-oriented manner.

Personal Pain Management Plans

Creating personalized pain management plans marks a critical step in the somatic approach to chronic pain. These plans can be co-created by individuals and their therapists and tailored to the unique contours of each person's experience with pain.

They incorporate various somatic techniques:

- Mindful movement

- Breathwork

- Relaxation and body awareness practices

These plans also account for the individual's daily routines and responsibilities, ensuring the techniques chosen are effective, practical, and sustainable.

Creating and implementing these plans involves regular check-ins and adjustments based on the individual's responses and evolving needs. This flexibility ensures the plan remains relevant and practical, a living document that guides the individual's journey through chronic pain.

The benefits of mindful movement practices, such as yoga or qi gong:

- Reduce pain intensity

- Improve physical function

- Enhance the quality of life for individuals with various chronic pain conditions

Studies on breathwork have highlighted its potential to:

- Reduce pain

- Alleviate stress

- Improve emotional well-being

Somatic therapy creates a holistic approach to pain management, one that honors the complexity of chronic pain and the uniqueness of each individual's experience.

In this approach, chronic pain is a part of the self to be understood and cared for. It invites a shift in perspective from seeing the body as a source of suffering to recognizing it as a partner in healing. It's about rediscovering a sense of wholeness and well-being, even in the presence of pain.

Somatic Therapy for Improved Sleep

During the peaceful hours of the night, when the surrounding world quiets down, the search for sleep can sometimes feel like a lonely journey through the mind's whispers and the body's restlessness. However, helpful practices are available that can turn the bed from a place of insomnia struggles into a calming sanctuary for restful surrender. By weaving together movements and breaths, the body can find a rhythm that aligns with the soothing pace of the night, allowing sleep to come gently and peacefully.

Somatic Exercises for Sleep

Initiating practices tailored for sleep begins with the breath, the body's natural lullaby, whose rhythms can soothe the jagged edges of a weary mind.

The following breathing method mimics the respiratory patterns of deep sleep, coaxing the nervous system into a calm state.

- **The 4-7-8 Breathing Method:** Inhale for four counts, hold for seven, and exhale for eight.

Stretches to release the day's accumulations from the body's nooks serve as a prelude to sleep and a ritual that cleanses and calms in equal measure.

- **Mindful Stretches:**

  - Slow neck rolls in each direction.

  - Slowly touch your toes, letting your torso, head, and arms hang loosely while breathing slowly and deeply.

  - Seated spinal twists, inhaling to lengthen your spine and exhaling while twisting gently to one side and then the other.

  - Standing side stretch: Reach both arms overhead with a nice deep breath in, then exhale and reach over to one side, returning to center and repeating on the other side.

The next practice is a method where attention is softly focused on various body parts, inviting each to relax, which becomes a dialogue of care.

- **"Body Whispering":**

  - Find a quiet space and get comfortable.

  - Close your eyes and take a few deep breaths to center yourself.

  - Bring your attention inward and begin to scan your body from head to toe, noticing any areas of tension, discomfort, or relaxation.

  - Tune into the subtle sensations of your body, such as tingling, warmth, or tightness.

  - Adopt a receptive and nonjudgmental attitude, allowing any sensations or messages to arise without trying to change or analyze them.

  - Focus on one area of your body, such as your shoulders, chest, or abdomen.

○ Explore the sensations in that area with curiosity, noticing any changes or shifts as you breathe and relax.

○ Respond to your body's signals, using gentle movements or self-massage to release tension and promote relaxation.

○ Honor any needs that arise, whether it's taking a break, stretching, or simply resting.

○ After the practice, take a moment to reflect on your experience and any insights gained.

This attentiveness to the physical self, acknowledging areas of tension and consciously releasing them, aligns the body's energies for rest, preparing the ground for deep, healing sleep.

Understanding Sleep Patterns

The exploration of sleep through somatic therapy delves into the intricacies of sleep patterns, acknowledging their susceptibility to the mind's churn and the body's unrest. This understanding illuminates the reciprocal relationship between sleep and somatic states, where disturbances in one ripple through the other. By charting the body's responses to various somatic exercises, individuals learn to discern the practices that harmonize their sleep patterns, aligning them closer to the natural cycles of light and dark that govern rest. This awareness becomes a compass, guiding the nightly voyage to the shores of peaceful sleep.

Before-Bed Routines

Creating a bedtime routine that incorporates somatic practices can be a work of art.

One routine could involve letting go of the day's stresses and tensions.

- **Mindful Movements:** Practice yoga or qi gong.

This link provides a video to improve sleep: https://www.youtube.com/wa tch?v=Qkzq1CvX1cQ

SCAN ME

- **Meditation:** Allow the mind to find peace in the rhythm of inhalation and exhalation.

- **A warm bath:** The water's embrace mimics the womb's safety.

By combining these practices, you can create a cozy and comforting environment that lets you let go of the day's stress and experience a serene and weightless feeling before drifting off to sleep.

A few years ago, I understood what it meant to have sleepless nights. Some nights I struggled to fall asleep; other times I would fall asleep immediately but wake up halfway through the night. I'd lay awake for hours, fidgeting and frustrated. I would finally fall asleep just to have to wake up for work an hour later. The days seemed endless, and each passing night only added to the exhaustion I was experiencing. Since creating my personal before-bed routine, I am thankful that I sleep amazingly well.

My routine involves slowing down one hour before bed. I make an effort to go to sleep at the same time every night. I take the hour before bed to check in with myself and see what kind of day I've had. I will do some gentle stretching with breathwork and a short gratitude meditation. Sometimes that is enough, but if I feel too much tension from my day, I will have a warm bath before stretching.

The 4-7-8 breathing method works well if I wake up in the middle of the night. I can count maybe three rounds, and then return to dreamland.

With the different methods we discussed, you will find the perfect fit through trial and error. Have patience, as the new sleep habits you will create are well worth the efforts you will put in.

Chapter 7: Tools and Techniques

Stress Management

- Progressive muscle relaxation

- Daily practices

  - Earthing

  - Focused stretching

  - Body scanning

Easing Anxiety and Panic Attacks

- 5-4-3-2-1 method

- Practice of containment

- Journal daily

- Incorporate regular somatic exercises

- Understand your triggers

- Incorporate mindfulness

- Regular physical activity

- Nutritional balance

Coping with Depression

- Mindful movements – Somatic yoga video: https://www.youtube.com/watch?v=Sxddnugwu-8

- Breathwork

- Stretching

- Community support

Addressing Chronic Pain

- Mindful movements – Somatic yoga video: https://www.youtube.com/watch?v=62k71bFeyOA

- Diaphragmatic breathing

Exercises for Improved Sleep

- 4-7-8 breathing method

- Mindful stretches

- Body whispering

- Mindful movements – Somatic yoga video: https://www.youtube.com/watch?v=Qkzq1CvX1cQ

- Meditation

- A warm bath

Chapter 8

Shaping a Lifelong Somatic Journey

Personalization and Progress Tracking

*"Your body is a living, breathing masterpiece. Treat it with love
and respect." – unknown*

The moments between each breath offer a valuable opportunity for personal growth and self-awareness. Despite being easily overlooked in our busy lives, these quiet spaces hold immense potential for those willing to listen and observe the subtle dialogue between the body and mind. By paying attention to the mutual influence of breath and movement, thought and sensation, we can tap into the innate wisdom of our bodies. Somatic practices are a powerful way to harness this wisdom, but it's essential to personalize them according to our unique needs, goals, and circumstances.

By sculpting practices that resonate with our individual lives, we can pave the way for a meaningful journey of growth and transformation.

Personalization of Practice

The art of tailoring somatic exercises is like a tailor adjusting a garment to the unique shape of their client. Just as no two bodies are identical, no two somatic practices should be identical.

The starting point is self-awareness, an intimate understanding of one's body, strengths, vulnerabilities, and language. Imagine stepping into a room filled with mirrors, each reflecting a different aspect of your being—physical, emotional, and mental. Observing these reflections without judgment allows one to discern the areas that crave movement, release, or perhaps stillness. This self-awareness is the foundation upon which personalized somatic practices are built.

Assessment Tools

Incorporating assessment tools into the personalization process offers a structured approach to understanding one's somatic landscape.

It can be as simple as a checklist that evaluates the following:

- Bodily awareness

- Emotional regulation

- Stress levels

By regularly completing this checklist, patterns emerge, revealing the somatic areas requiring attention and the exercises that might offer the most benefit. This systematic approach ensures that the practice remains aligned with evolving needs and goals, making each somatic session a step toward deeper self-knowledge and well-being.

Are you seeking to alleviate stress, enhance bodily awareness, or foster a deeper connection with your emotions?

Each intention will guide you toward specific practices that best suit your objectives.

Choose exercises that appeal to you, and accommodate any physical considerations, ensuring the routine remains accessible and enjoyable. For example, focusing on stress reduction may draw you toward breathwork and grounding exercises, while a desire for emotional connectivity might lead to mindful movement and expressive dance.

To tailor a practice that feels like a second skin:

- **Reflect on your daily flow.**

- **Identify spaces that naturally lend themselves to introspection and movement.**

- **Consider your goals.**

- **Factor in your preferences and limitations.**

Sample Routines

For a fast-paced lifestyle, a routine might look like this:

- A series of short, grounding practices scattered throughout the day.

- A morning breathwork session to set intentions.

- A midday body scan to recalibrate.

- An evening expressive movement practice to release the day's accumulation of stress.

For those with a more flexible schedule or a preference for depth:

- A longer morning session that combines meditation, yoga, and journaling might serve as a comprehensive practice that grounds, energizes, and introspects.

While distinct, each routine shares the intrinsic value of creating a structured yet fluid space for somatic engagement, anchoring you in a cycle of continuous presence and renewal.

Adapting Exercises

The fluid nature of life necessitates an adaptable approach to somatic exercises. Adaptation might mean modifying a posture to accommodate a physical limitation or adjusting the duration of practice to fit into a busy schedule.

It's about finding what works for you here and now. For instance, if lower back pain is a concern, adapting exercises to include gentle stretching and strengthening of the core might offer relief and support.

Similarly, when time is scarce, a five-minute focused breathing session can be a powerful tool for centering and calming the mind. The key is flexibility, an openness to modify practices as circumstances change, ensuring that somatic exercises remain a supportive and sustainable part of one's routine.

Adjusting over Time

As with all aspects of life, change is inevitable, and the effectiveness of your somatic routine will change with the shifting tides of your circumstances, needs, and insights.

Regular reflection on the resonance of your practice is crucial. Ask yourself the following questions:

- Does this still serve my highest good?

- What feels lacking, and how can I adjust to fulfill this need?

Perhaps new challenges or insights have emerged, prompting a shift in focus or the introduction of new exercises. Or maybe certain practices no longer elicit the same depth of engagement and must be replaced.

Embracing these adjustments with openness and flexibility allows your routine to evolve harmoniously with your personal growth, ensuring it remains a vital source of support and enrichment.

Feedback Loops

Creating feedback loops within the practice of somatic exercises ensures a dynamic, responsive approach to personal growth and healing.

This involves a conscious reflection after each session, noting, for example:

- Any physical sensations

- Emotional shifts

- Insights that arise

Questions to ask yourself:

- What did I notice?

- How did I feel?

- Where was resistance encountered?

- Where was ease found?

They serve as keys to unlocking the deeper significance of these experiences.

Feedback loops invite an ongoing dialogue with the body, a question-and-answer session where the body's responses guide the evolution of the practice. This reflective process fosters a deepened connection with oneself, making somatic exercises a practice and a way of life.

Crafting a somatic routine that resonates with your individual rhythms and needs demands a thoughtful approach that honors the uniqueness of your lived experience and aspirations. This endeavor requires not just an understanding of various somatic practices but also a deep listening to one's body and mind, discerning what truly nourishes and aligns with your personal journey toward well-being.

Tracking Progress

Monitoring the evolution of your somatic journey offers invaluable insights into the impact of your routine and areas ripe for refinement.

This can be achieved through various means such as:

- **Maintaining a Journal:**

    - Document your daily practices and their immediate effects.

    - Note shifts in your relationship with your body.

    - Note changes in emotional resilience.

    - Note enhancements in your capacity for presence.

- **Setting Periodic Check-Ins with Yourself:** Assess longer-term changes in your well-being, stress levels, and bodily awareness.

- **Revisiting the Initial Assessment Tools:** Compare results over time to gauge progress.

These reflective practices become mirrors of the evolving relationship between body and mind, revealing patterns, illuminating breakthroughs, and uncovering areas ripe for further exploration. They provide a nuanced understanding of your routine's effectiveness.

Creating a personalized routine is a testament to our commitment to self-discovery and healing. Through thoughtful personalization, the exploration of sample routines, the willingness to adjust to changing needs, and the diligent tracking of progress, we create a practice that deeply resonates with our individual journeys. This process, rich with introspection and adaptation, ensures that our somatic routines remain dynamic reflections of our evolving selves, offering continuous support and nourishment as we move through life. With each step, we affirm our dedication to cultivating a harmonious relationship between body and mind, unlocking new depths of awareness and well-being.

The practices we cultivate transform our individual lives and ripple outward, influencing our interactions with others and our engagement with the world. This realization underscores the profound impact of our somatic journeys, inviting us to continue exploring with curiosity, openness, and a deep sense of purpose.

Lifelong Somatic Practice

Keeping the Journey Alive

As the body weathers the storms of change—physical transformations, emotional upheavals, and shifts in the landscape of daily life—the practice must morph, embracing these changes with grace and resilience. This morphing is not a sign of inconsistency but a testament to the practice's vitality and capacity to breathe and evolve with the individual.

To sustain this vibrant practice, one might find solace and strength in routines that anchor the day, morning stretching gestures that greet the dawn with openness, or nightly rituals of grounding that whisper tales of gratitude to the twilight. Yet, within these routines, a space for spontaneity ensures the practice remains vibrant and alive to the moment's call, whether it calls for the need of vigorous movement or the stillness of meditation.

Listening carefully and being attuned to subtle shifts and changes is essential. This may mean reducing the intensity of the practice as the body ages and recognizing and accepting the stories imprinted on the body's lines and contours. Or, it might reveal itself in exploring new somatic territories as life circumstances shift—an openness to the unfamiliar that invigorates the practice with fresh insights and energies.

Amid this personal exploration, the importance of continued growth within somatic therapy stands as a pillar. Collaborative learning experiences such as workshops, retreats, and conversations with fellow seekers can serve as sources of inspiration, nurturing one's practice with the collective knowledge and experiences of the community. In this pursuit of growth, the practice deepens, branching out in new directions, enriched by the nutrients of learning and the light of exploration.

At the heart of sustaining a lifelong somatic practice lies the desire to incorporate the wisdom of somatic living into one's own life and the lives of others, thereby creating a lasting legacy. This legacy, crafted with our experience and personal insight, offers a mosaic of knowledge to those who walk the path alongside and after us. In this sense, teaching becomes an act of sharing, a generous offering of the fruits harvested from one's somatic explorations. Whether through formal instruction or the subtle teachings embodied in one's way of being, this legacy plants seeds of somatic awareness in the garden of the collective consciousness, ensuring that the wisdom of the body continues to flourish, generation after generation.

Chapter 8: Tools and Techniques

Create a Personal Somatic Routine

- Reflect on your daily flow

- Identify your space

- Consider your goals

- Factor in your exercise preferences

Track Your Progress

- Maintain a journal

- Set periodic check-ins with yourself

- Revisit the initial assessment tools

Chapter 9

BONUS - Empowering the Self

Navigating Inner Landscapes and Relationships Through Somatic Practices

As the day ends and the world grows quieter, we often find a unique opportunity to explore our inner selves. Our emotions and psychological depths create an intricate terrain that can be challenging to navigate. However, somatic therapy, deeply rooted in the body's wisdom, can provide a map to help us explore this inner world. By using the sensations and cues of our body as a compass, we can navigate the intricate pathways of our inner landscapes, uncovering insights and treasures that lie beneath the surface.

Exploring Inner Landscapes

In somatic therapy, exploring one's inner landscape begins with the body. It's like walking through a dense forest, where each step and breath brings a new discovery and understanding of the land and oneself. The body holds the keys to unlocking these inner realms in its infinite wisdom. Through movements, breaths, and sensations, we learn to read the subtle signs and signals that guide us deeper into our emotional and psychological terrains.

A moment as simple as noticing the tension in one's shoulders while waiting in line at the café and then consciously relaxing them can serve as an entry point into a deeper understanding of the sources of stress and how they manifest in the body. This awareness, cultivated over time, allows us to navigate our inner landscapes more efficiently, connecting physical sensations and emotional states and uncovering the underlying patterns that shape our experiences and behaviors.

Self-Awareness Exercises

Somatic therapy offers a suite of exercises designed to heighten self-awareness, each acting as a tool to excavate and examine the layers of the self.

One exercise involves the following:

- **The Practice of Stillness:**

    - Sit or lie down in a comfortable position.

    - Close your eyes and bring attention to the breath, noticing its rhythm and texture.

    - Expand your awareness to encompass the body, noting any sensations, tensions, or discomforts without judgment.

This practice, repeated regularly, sharpens the senses to the body's language, turning every sensation into a word, and every tension into a sentence in the ongoing narrative of our inner selves.

Reflective Practices

Interconnected with these exercises are reflective practices that deepen the journey of self-discovery.

- **Keep a Somatic Journal:** Record not just thoughts and emotions but bodily sensations and their fluctuations.

Questions like:

- When did I feel most alive today?

- What is my body trying to tell me through this tension?

They prompt a dialogue between body and mind, revealing insights that might remain obscured.

This reflection extends beyond the journal, infusing daily life with mindfulness and curiosity. It transforms mundane activities into opportunities for self-discovery, whether noticing the emotional shifts during a walk in the park or the sensations accompanying a moment of laughter or tears. Through this lens, every moment becomes a potential for insight and transformation.

Shared Experiences

My friend, Jane, is a fantastic artist, but at times she would become paralyzed by self-doubt and criticism, completely blocking her creativity. For her, a particular somatic exercise of moving to music that felt authentic and unrestrained broke open the floodgates, allowing her creativity to flow freely. Her art and relationship with herself transformed, growing richer and more nuanced.

One of my former colleagues, who is a high-level executive, found a way to navigate through a period of intense burnout and stress through somatic therapy. For him, grounding, feeling the earth beneath his feet, and imagining roots extending deep into the ground became a daily ritual that restored his sense of balance and presence. Over time, this practice alleviated his stress and deepened his capacity for empathy and connection, reshaping his approach to leadership and interpersonal relationships. I was so happy for him when he shared his story with me. I can't get enough of hearing people's success stories when they invest time and energy into their personal well-being.

In this exploration, we find the shadows and complexities of our inner worlds and the light and potential that reside there. Somatic therapy, with its grounding in the wisdom of the body, offers a way to navigate this terrain with grace and insight, turning every step and every breath into an opportunity for growth and discovery.

Somatics for Strengthening Relationships

Many elements tie us together in the complex web of human relationships, including empathy, understanding, and intimacy. Nurturing these qualities requires a deep understanding of the unspoken cues in our nonverbal communication. Somatic practices offer powerful tools to strengthen our connections with others and improve our communication skills.

Empathy and Connection

Empathy can transform personal experience into a bridge toward understanding another's emotional state. This transformation begins in somatic awareness, where tuning into one's bodily sensations becomes a channel for tuning into another's feelings. Imagine the sensation of a heart racing in response to a partner's distress or the warmth in one's hands as they reach out in comfort. When observed and understood, these bodily responses act as empathetic resonances, aligning one's emotional state with that of another, and fostering a connection beyond words.

This resonance is about mirroring and genuinely inhabiting the space of another's experience, if only for a moment. By grounding oneself in somatic awareness, one becomes more adept at discerning the subtle shifts in another's posture, the unspoken tensions that speak of unvoiced concerns, or the slight tremble that hints at underlying excitement. When met with an open heart and a receptive body, these somatic cues pave the way for genuine empathy, breaking down barriers and nurturing a connection rooted in mutual understanding.

Communicating Through the Body

The body speaks its own language. It can convey meaning in ways that words cannot. Communicating through this somatic language opens new avenues for expression and understanding in relationships. It begins with a conscious engagement with one's own bodily sensations, recognizing them as messengers of emotional states and intentions.

- A clenched jaw might reveal suppressed frustration.

- An open stance may signal a willingness to connect.

- A gentle touch can convey support and presence.

- A deep, synchronized breath can bring alignment and calm to a heated conversation.

- Consciously relaxing one's body can signal openness and receptivity.

With this awareness, individuals can intentionally use their bodies to communicate feelings and needs, inviting similar openness from others.

This somatic dialogue, subtle yet profound, enhances verbal communication, adding depth and authenticity to the exchange and strengthening the bond between individuals.

Conflict Resolution Techniques

Conflict, while often seen as a disruptor of harmony, can also catalyze growth and deeper understanding within relationships. Somatic practices offer tools for navigating conflicts with grace, using the body's wisdom to move through tension toward resolution.

Before engaging in a difficult conversation, use the following technique to calm the nervous system and create a physical and emotional space to address conflicts with clarity and composure.

- **Grounding:** Take a moment to feel your feet firmly planted on the earth and take deep breaths to center yourself.

Using the somatic self-regulation technique, you can help de-escalate rising emotions and influence the emotional tone of the interaction, steering it toward calm and constructive dialogue.

- **Somatic Self-Regulation:** Slow your breathing to lower the heart rate.

Building Intimacy

At the heart of every meaningful relationship lies the treasure of intimacy, a closeness that brings individuals together in shared trust and vulnerability. Somatic practices enrich this bond, offering exercises that deepen connections through shared bodily experiences.

The synchronized breathing exercises can align partners in a rhythm of mutual presence, a simple yet profound act of togetherness.

- **Synchronized Breathing Exercises:**

    - Coordinate breath patterns by inhaling and exhaling in unison, following a set rhythm, promoting relaxation, connection, and synchronization.

- **Mindful Touch:**

    - Focus on the sensations and emotions arising from gentle, intentional contact.

    - Focus on sensations, textures, and pressure during physical contact.

    - Approach touch with intention and sensitivity to the other person's needs and boundaries.

When used in daily interactions, these practices nurture a deep sense of connection and affection and bind individuals closer, not just through shared experiences but through a mutual attunement to the somatic undercurrents that flow between them. This attunement fosters an intimacy that is not only physical but emotional and spiritual, a confluence of connections that nurtures the relationship at every level.

In this exploration of somatics for strengthening relationships, the body emerges as a bridge toward a deeper connection with others. Through empathy and understanding, communicated through the subtle language of bodily sensations and cues, individuals can navigate conflicts with grace and nurture intimacy with intention. In this dance of connection, somatic practices offer steps to follow and a rhythm to live by, a melody that guides us closer to one another, rich with depth, understanding, and love.

Somatics to Overcome Limiting Beliefs

Our thoughts and experiences weave intricate patterns within us, shaping the stories we tell ourselves. Unfortunately, some of these stories are limiting beliefs that hold us back from realizing our full potential. These beliefs are deeply rooted in our minds and often find expression in our bodies as physical tension, such as a tight shoulder or a constricted chest. However, there are somatic practices that can help us uncover and release these hidden beliefs, replacing them with more empowering narratives that expand our sense of self. We can gently untangle these limiting beliefs with patience and compassion and create a more luminous path forward.

Identifying Limiting Beliefs

The initial step on this transformative path involves illuminating these shadowy beliefs. It begins with a somatic dialogue, tuning into the body's whispers and roars.

Focused body scans, where attention meanders through the body, pausing to listen to its tales, serve as a lantern in the dark, revealing the hiding spots of these beliefs. A sudden tightness in the belly when contemplating success, a quickened pulse at the thought of intimacy—each is a clue, a breadcrumb leading back to a core limiting belief.

- **Body Scanning:** Lie still, close your eyes, and direct your attention to each part of your body. Notice the sensations that dwell within—tension, warmth, discomfort, or ease.

This process requires patience as the body communicates with us through sensations and emotions, which require us to tune in to its subtle frequencies.

Releasing Techniques

With these beliefs brought into the light, the work of release begins. The somatic approach adopts a physicality that mirrors the emotional and psychological unburdening it aims to achieve.

- **Dynamic Movements**: Use slow qi gong movements or expressive dance flows to allow the body to shake loose the grip of these limiting beliefs.

As muscles unwind and breath deepens, space is created for new narratives to seed and grow.

- **Guided Visualization:** Invite the mind to construct scenarios of freedom and possibility.

The body actively participates in unshackling old narratives through these practices, a vessel for transformation.

Reprogramming the Mind-Body

The void left by discarding a limiting belief is fertile ground for planting empowering beliefs and narratives. This reprogramming of the mind-body connection is similar to cultivating a garden. Just as a gardener selects seeds carefully, so must we choose the beliefs we wish to grow within us.

- **Affirmations:** Repeat a phrase as simple as "I am worthy of love and belonging" with intention while embodying this truth through posture and breath.

This begins to reroute the neural pathways previously dominated by limiting beliefs. Potent seeds of thought are planted through repetition and embodiment. Over time, this practice nurtures the growth of empowering beliefs, eventually blossoming into actions and experiences that reflect this new narrative.

Success Frameworks

The terrain of success, often perceived as rugged and daunting, becomes navigable with the map provided by somatic practices. Frameworks for achieving goals by overcoming limiting beliefs through these practices are constructed of fluid, adaptable strategies. They reinforce empowering beliefs and facilitate a deepening connection with the body's wisdom. They serve as a scaffolding, supporting the individual as they climb toward their goals.

The key to success is:

- **A Somatic Routine:** Establish a somatic routine and a daily engagement with practices.

- **Periodic Reflection:** Assess progress and realign actions with intentions.

Just as a navigator periodically checks their compass to ensure they are on course, we must pause to consider our alignment with our desired trajectory. This reflection is somatically grounded, checking in with the body to sense congruence or discord with our path and adjusting accordingly.

Collectively, these strategies provide a web of support, guiding individuals through the maze of their own limiting beliefs toward the realization of their potential. Through the somatic lens, success is redefined as a landscape to be explored and savored, with each step informed by the body's wisdom and the spirit's resilience.

Cultivating Inner Strength and Confidence

We all face challenges in life that test our self-assurance and inner fortitude. These challenges require us to develop resilience and courage to navigate through them. However, this process of personal growth often requires nurturing through practices that focus on the body and its sensations. Somatic therapy is a powerful tool that can help us transform and cultivate lasting inner strength and confidence, like a garden of flourishing plants that never wither away.

Building Inner Strength

The power of embodied practices is undeniable, as they allow us to build a strong and resilient foundation of inner strength. By engaging in a dialogue with our body, we can tap into the deep reservoirs of strength within us. This dialogue helps us unveil the potential for strength within us, often hidden beneath layers of self-doubt and hesitation.

Mindfully observing our breath and bodily sensations strengthens our presence and helps us stay grounded in our solidity.

Through this grounding, we can uncover the bedrock of our inner strength, which allows us to rise above our vulnerabilities. Cultivating this strength requires practices that engage the body in its entirety.

- **Grounding:** Visualize roots extending from the soles of the feet deep into the earth.

This rootedness offers stability and resilience and becomes a source of strength from which confidence can draw, nourished by the solidity of our connection to the ground beneath us.

Confidence-Boosting Practices

Confidence, often mistaken as a quality bestowed upon a fortunate few, is a garden cultivated through intentional practice, where somatic therapy offers the tools for its nurture. Practices designed to boost confidence work by aligning body, breath, and intention, creating a harmonious symphony that resonates with self-assurance.

- **Postural Adjustments:** Stand tall, with your shoulders relaxed yet open.

We embody confidence, sending signals to the brain that reflect this stance, a feedback loop that elevates our sense of self. This is to alter our physical presence and shift our internal landscapes.

- **Diaphragmatic Breathing:** Focus on the rise and fall of your belly during each inhalation and exhalation.

This technique calms the nervous system, reducing the physiological markers of anxiety and fear. This calmness lays the ground for confidence to emerge, a quiet certainty that stems not from arrogance but from a deep-seated belief in one's capabilities and worth.

Overcoming Fear

Fear, with its icy grip, can paralyze, turning potential pathways into impassable canyons. Somatic therapy, however, offers a torch to light the way through this fog, to help navigate our fears with grace.

The physical manifestations of fear:

- A quickened heartbeat

- Tense muscles

- Shallow breathing

By acknowledging fear, we begin to demystify its power, recognizing it as a natural response rather than an insurmountable obstacle.

- **Progressive Muscle Relaxation:** Apply tension to different muscle groups and then release it. (Explained in detail in Chapter 4.)

This somatic approach to fear does not aim to eradicate it but to transform our relationship with it, to see it as a signpost rather than a roadblock. It teaches the body a new way of being, where fear can be acknowledged and then let go. Through this transformation, fear becomes a catalyst for growth, a challenge to be met with the inner strength and confidence we have nurtured.

Empowerment Journey

Through somatic therapy, I have discovered the courage to voice my dreams aloud and to step into the light of my aspirations with unwavering confidence. For me, the journey involved the physical practices of somatic therapy and the introspective work of aligning my somatic experiences with my deepest values and desires. Once achieved, this alignment became the compass by which I navigated my journey, marked by the presence of courage.

I have also reclaimed my voice in a world that had long silenced me. Through exercises that grounded me in my body, I found the strength to stand firm in my truth and to express myself with clarity and confidence. This newfound empowerment transformed my relationships and perception of myself—a transformation that began in the body but resonated through every facet of my life.

I share my journey to demonstrate the profound impact of somatic therapy in cultivating inner strength and confidence. Through the embodied practices of somatic therapy, we learn to navigate the landscapes of fear and doubt, to plant and nurture the seeds of confidence, and to harvest the fruits of empowerment.

This intensely personal yet universally resonant process is a testament to the transformative power of connecting with our bodies, listening to their wisdom, and allowing that wisdom to guide us toward our most empowered selves.

Somatics for Mindful Eating and Body Image

The morning sunlight seeps through the curtains, casting a gentle glow on the breakfast table. In these peaceful moments, we have an opportunity to practice mindful eating. This practice goes beyond just consuming food and becomes a ritual of gratitude and presence.

By taking a somatic approach to eating, we can connect with our senses and develop a deeper appreciation for our food. Every bite and every texture becomes a moment of connection with our body's needs and desires.

- **Intentional Engagement:** Savor every flavor and pay attention to your hunger and satiety cues.

This creates a harmonious relationship with food based on our body's wisdom rather than the external pressures of diet culture. Many people struggle with body image due to societal pressures and internalized feelings of inadequacy. However, somatic therapy can provide a source of healing. It involves reclaiming the body from objectification and viewing it as an ally rather than an object.

- **Appreciate the Body:** Focus on the body's capabilities, resilience, and grace for what it can do rather than how it looks.

This appreciation is nurtured through practices like the following:

- **Yoga or Dance:** Create a positive relationship with your body by enhancing bodily awareness and shifting the focus from external validation to internal acceptance.

- **Nutritional Awareness:** Shift your focus from the quantitative aspects of eating—calories, grams, percentages—to the qualitative experience of nourishing the body.

This shift, facilitated by practices that encourage tuning into the body's signals of hunger and fullness, leads to a more intuitive approach to eating. It respects the body's innate wisdom, choosing foods that satisfy both taste and the body's nutritional needs, fostering vitality and well-being.

The following techniques have proven to be helpful to those struggling with body image:

- **Body Scanning:** Lie still, close your eyes, and direct your attention to each part of your body. Notice the sensations that dwell within—tension, warmth, discomfort, or ease, including sensations related to hunger and fullness.

- **Yoga:** Practice mindful movement through yoga postures to help connect with bodily sensations related to hunger and fullness.

- **Diaphragmatic Breathing:** Focus on the rise and fall of your belly during each inhalation and exhalation in order to become more attuned to bodily sensations, including hunger and fullness cues.

- **Progressive Muscle Relaxation:** Apply tension to different muscle groups and then release it. (Explained in detail in Chapter 4.) This helps promote body awareness, which can help individuals tune into their body's signals, including hunger and fullness.

- **Somatic Experiencing:** Focus on releasing bodily tension and trauma to promote greater awareness of bodily sensations, including hunger and fullness. (Explained in detail in Chapter 6)

- **Mindful Eating Exercises:**

  - Eat slowly, savoring each bite and chewing thoroughly.

  - Notice the colors, textures, smells, and tastes of the food.

  - Pay attention to physical hunger cues and satiety signals.

  - Eat without distractions such as screens or reading material.

  - Approach food with curiosity and without judgment or guilt.

  - Cultivate gratitude for the food and those involved in its production.

  - Serve yourself appropriate portions and be mindful of portion sizes.

  - Pause midway through the meal to check in with hunger and fullness levels.

  - Practice mindful eating during select meals or snacks throughout the day.

  - Reflect on the experience afterward, noting any insights or observations about eating habits and preferences.

These exercises can help individuals become more attuned to their body's hunger and fullness signals. Like other common challenges, finding what works for your body daily is the key. Think about which combination of techniques resonates with you and how you can incorporate them into your daily routine. Consistency is the only way to begin reaping the benefits.

The therapeutic potential of somatic practices in navigating the complex terrain of body image and eating reminds us that at the heart of these practices lies a simple yet profound truth: the body, with its intricate wisdom and capacity for joy, is not an adversary to be controlled but a companion to be cherished. Through mindful eating and a compassionate engagement with our bodies, we learn to nourish not just the physical self but the entirety of our being, fostering a state of harmony and well-being that radiates from within.

An intricate dance between the body and the mind plays out in how we nourish ourselves, perceive our bodies, and move through the world. In their gentle wisdom, somatic practices guide us through this dance, teaching us to listen to the body's cues, honor its needs, and celebrate its beauty. In embracing these practices, we embrace a more compassionate, mindful, and joyful way of being, setting the stage for a deeper exploration of the self and the world around us.

Chapter 9: Tools and Techniques

Self-Awareness Practice

- Practice of stillness

- Keep a somatic journal

Conflict Resolution

- Grounding

- Somatic self-regulation

Building Intimacy

- Synchronized breathing exercises

- Mindful touch

Overcoming Limiting Beliefs

- Body scanning

- Dynamic movements

- Guided visualization

- Affirmations

- Somatic routine

- Periodic reflection

Cultivating Inner Strength and Confidence

- Grounding

- Postural adjustments

- Diaphragmatic breathing

- Progressive muscle relaxation

Mindful Eating and Body Image

Somatic Approach

- Intentional engagement

- Focusing on the body's capabilities, resilience, and grace

- Yoga or dance

- Nutritional awareness

Techniques

- Body scanning

- Yoga

- Diaphragmatic breathing

- Progressive muscle relaxation

- Somatic experiencing

- Mindful eating exercises

- Create a daily routine

Share Your Journey – Help Others Find Their Path

My goal is to make this valuable resource available to everyone, and you can help!

If you haven't had a chance yet, I'd like to invite you to write a review on Amazon. Your voice matters—let it echo in the hearts of those searching for healing, just as you were.

Your review could help someone:

- Recover from trauma; Cultivate self-compassion; Rediscover joy

- Strengthen relationships; Reduce panic attacks; Break free from limiting beliefs

- And so much more!

Your kindness and willingness to share your thoughts are sincerely appreciated!

Click here to leave your review on Amazon – https://www.amazon.com/review/review-your-purchases/?asin=B0D974BLTZ

SCAN ME

"If you have knowledge, let others light their candles in it."– Margaret Fuller

Conclusion

Hey there,

Suppose you've made it to this point: Wow, just wow! I want to take a moment to truly celebrate you. Diving deep into somatic therapy, exploring your inner world, and committing to practices that might have felt unfamiliar or challenging at first—take courage—real courage. You've shown incredible bravery and dedication on this journey of self-discovery and healing. So, before anything else, give yourself a big pat on the back. You deserve it.

Throughout our time together on these pages, we've navigated some foundational principles of somatic therapy. We revisited the power of being truly present in our bodies, understanding the neurobiology of trauma and healing, and explored transformative techniques like breathwork, pendulation, titration, and resourcing. Each concept and technique we covered is a stepping stone toward fostering a deeper connection between your mind and body. Remember, this isn't just about learning; it's about transforming.

I hope you've grasped the core message: Somatic therapy is an incredibly powerful tool. It's there for you, whether you're looking to manage day-to-day stress, build resilience in the face of life's curveballs, or embark on a journey of recovery from past traumas. With the exercises and insights we've shared, you're now equipped to face your wellness journey with a newfound confidence. That's huge and I'm so proud of you for taking these steps.

But here's the thing: The transformative potential of somatic therapy doesn't stop with individual healing. It ripples out, touching our relationships and the very fabric of our lives. Imagine carrying this sense of presence, this deep connection to yourself, into your interactions with others. The possibilities for growth and understanding are boundless.

As we come to a close, I want to encourage you to keep going. The end of this book isn't the end of your exploration. Keep practicing, be open to discovering new techniques, and don't hesitate to seek out communities or professionals who can guide you further. There's a whole world of somatic therapy out there waiting for you.

And, if you feel moved to share your journey, your experiences and insights could light the way for others, spreading awareness and support for somatic therapy far and wide. Imagine the impact we could make together.

Thank you for trusting me to be a part of your journey. Remember, you're not alone in this. I'm with you, cheering you on every step of the way. This book and the practices within it are here for you, always.

As we part ways (for now), I want to leave you with this: Be kind to yourself. Healing and growth are journeys, not destinations. They take time, patience, and heaps of self-compassion. Trust in the process and your incredible capacity for resilience and transformation. I believe in you.

Here's to your journey, to your healing, and to the amazing path of discovery that lies ahead. May this book be both a signal of hope and a practical guide as you continue to navigate the beautiful, complex landscape of your inner world.

With all my support and heartfelt encouragement,

K. D. Anne

Ongoing Resources

If you are interested in discovering more about somatic therapy, here are some extra resources that might be helpful to you.

Somatic Experiencing Practitioners Near You

Somatic Experiencing International: https://directory.traumahealing.org/

SCAN ME

Podcast

https://rickhanson.com/being-well-podcast/

SCAN ME

Somatic Exercise App

https://neurofit.app/

References

"12 Effective Somatic Therapy Exercises for Holistic Healing," October 7, 2023. https://www.monakirstein.com/somatic-therapy-exercises/

"How to Rewire Your Brain: 6 Neuroplasticity Exercises." Healthline, June 17, 2020. https://www.healthline.com/health/rewiring-your-brain

"Somatics for Children: Helping Little Ones Thrive | Albert Wong," March 4, 2023. https://www.somatopia.com/blog/somatic-practices-children

"Somatics: Definition, Exercises, Evidence, and More." Healthline, April 17, 2020. https://www.healthline.com/health/somatics

"Want to Fix Your Mind? Let Your Body Talk." *The New York Times*, May 18, 2023, sec. Magazine. https://www.nytimes.com/2023/05/18/magazine/somatic-therapy.html

Arida, Ricardo Mario, and Lavinia Teixeira-Machado. "The Contribution of Physical Exercise to Brain Resilience." *Frontiers in Behavioral Neuroscience* 14 (January 20, 2021): 626769. https://doi.org/10.3389/fnbeh.2020.626769

Bergner, Daniel. "Want to Fix Your Mind? Let Your Body Talk." *The New York Times*, May 18, 2023, sec. Magazine. https://www.nytimes.com/2023/05/18/magazine/somatic-therapy.html

Boyd, Jenna E., Ruth A. Lanius, and Margaret C. McKinnon. "Mindfulness-Based Treatments for Posttraumatic Stress Disorder: A Review of the Treatment Literature and Neurobiological Evidence." *Journal of Psychiatry & Neuroscience : JPN* 43, no. 1 (January 2018): 7–25. https://doi.org/10.1503/jpn.170021

Center for Substance Abuse Treatment (US). "Understanding the Impact of Trauma." In *Trauma-Informed Care in Behavioral Health Services.* Substance Abuse and Mental Health Services Administration (US), 2014. https://www.ncbi.nlm.nih.gov/books/NBK207191/

Dodson, Julie. "A Guide: What Is Somatic Therapy?," December 6, 2023. https://www.betterhelp.com/

DuBois, Russell. "Integrating Technology into Mental Healthcare," n.d. https://www.psychotherapy.net/article/integrating-technology

Fowler, Paige. "Breathing Techniques for Stress Relief." WebMD, n.d. https://www.webmd.com/balance/stress-management/stress-relief-breathing-techniques

Gan, Ruochen, Liuyi Zhang, and Shulin Chen. "The Effects of Body Scan Meditation: A Systematic Review and Meta-analysis." *Applied Psychology: Health and Well-Being* 14, no. 3 (August 2022): 1062–80. https://doi.org/10.1111/aphw.12366

Gillett, Jenna. "Somatic Practice and Chronic Pain," January 27, 2021. https://warwick.ac.uk/fac/sci/psych/research/lifespan/sleeplab/projects/within/blog/january2021/#:~:text=Somatic%20practice%20uses%20the%20mind,have%20knowledge%20of%20chronic%20pain

Hanson, Heidi. "On The Importance of Titration for Trauma Healing (10 Benefits) - The Art of Healing Trauma," May 28, 2016. https://www.new-synapse.com/aps/wordpress/?p=1842

Jensen-Doss, Amanda, Emily M. Becker Haimes, Ashley M. Smith, Aaron R. Lyon, Cara C. Lewis, Cameo F. Stanick, and Kristin M. Hawley. "Monitoring Treatment Progress and Providing Feedback Is Viewed Favorably but Rarely Used in Practice." *Administration and Policy in Mental Health* 45, no. 1 (January 2018): 48–61. https://doi.org/10.1007/s10488-016-0763-0

Jonathan. "Ethical Consideration in Somatic Psychotherapies." *Bodynamic International* (blog), October 14, 2017. https://www.bodynamic.com/blog/ethical-consideration-in-somatic-psychotherapies/

Kamp, Minke M. van de, Mia Scheffers, Janneke Hatzmann, Claudia Emck, Pim Cuijpers, and Peter J. Beek. "Body- and Movement-Oriented Interventions for Posttraumatic Stress Disorder: A Systematic Review and Meta-Analysis." *Journal of Traumatic Stress* 32, no. 6 (December 2019): 967–76. https://doi.org/10.1002/jts.22465

Kirstein, Mona and Ph.D. "7 Best Somatic Breathwork Exercises for Stress-Relief," November 2, 2023. https://www.monakirstein.com/somatic-breathwork/

Kuhfuß, Marie, Tobias Maldei, Andreas Hetmanek, and Nicola Baumann. "Somatic Experiencing – Effectiveness and Key Factors of a Body-Oriented Trauma Therapy: A Scoping Literature Review." *European Journal of Psychotraumatology* 12, no. 1 (n.d.): 1929023. https://doi.org/10.1080/20008198.2021.1929023

LPC, Michelle Wegman. "Emotional Safety: What It Is and How to Develop It." The Counseling Collective, April 4, 2023. https://www.discovercounselingcollective.com/blog/2023/2/5/emotional-safety-what-it-is-and-how-to-develop-it

Marklew, Jade. "The Benefits of Breathwork for Emotional Regulation." *Mana Health Clinic* (blog), June 6, 2023. https://manahealthclinic.com.au/the-benefits-of-breathwork-for-emotional-regulation/

McKean, Briony. "Overcoming Barriers to Self-Care." *Psychologist Gold Coast - CBT Professionals* (blog), July 27, 2023. https://cbtprofessionals.com.au/overcoming-barriers-to-self-care/

MeditationMind. "The Complete Guide to Somatic Meditation," January 1, 2023. https://meditationfocused.com/somatic-meditation/

MPH, Alex Bachert. "Try These Somatic Exercises to Improve Your Mental Health." Charlie Health, August 2, 2023. https://www.charliehealth.com/post/somatic-exercises-for-mental-health

NSF. "Mind-Body Connection Is Built into Brain, Study Suggests," May 23, 2023. https://new.nsf.gov/news/mind-body-connection-built-brain-study-suggests

Ph.D, Anna Katharina Schaffner. "How to Perform Somatic Coaching: 9 Best Exercises." PositivePsychology.com, November 14, 2023. https://positivepsychology.com/somatic-coaching/

Ph.D, Melissa Madeson. "Embodiment Practices: How to Heal Through Movement." PositivePsychology.com, August 11, 2021. https://positivepsychology.com/embodiment-philosophy-practices/

Ramirez-Duran, Daniela. "Somatic Experiencing Therapy: 10 Best Exercises & Examples." PositivePsychology.com, November 11, 2020. https://positivepsychology.com/somatic-experiencing/

Raypole, Crystal. "30 Grounding Techniques: Exercises for Anxiety, PTSD, and More." Healthline, May 24, 2019. https://www.healthline.com/health/grounding-techniques

Ross, Sarah. "Resourcing, Pendulation and Titration: Practices from So-matic Experiencing®." *Psychotherapy for Women, Families, and Children in Berkeley, CA* (blog), January 3, 2018. https://sarahrossphd.com/re-sourcing-pendulation-titration-practices-somatic-experiencing/

Russo, Marc A., Danielle M. Santarelli, and Dean O'Rourke. "The Physiological Effects of Slow Breathing in the Healthy Human." *Breathe* 13, no. 4 (December 2017): 298–309. https://doi.org/10.1183/20734735.009817

Stephanie Mara. "The History of Somatics: The Pioneers," June 25, 2023. https://www.stephaniemara.com/blog/the-history-of-somat-ics-the-pioneers

Team Neurofit. "3 Somatic Exercises to Support a Good Night's Sleep - NEUROFIT." NEUROFIT, n.d. https://neurofit.app/blog/posts/3-so-matic-exercises-to-support-a-good-nights-sleep

Warren, Sarah. "Developing Your Own Daily Practice." *Somatic Move-ment Center* (blog), February 1, 2023. https://somaticmovementcen-ter.com/daily-practice/

Wong, Dr. Albert. "Neuroscience of Somatic Psychology," June 21, 2023. https://www.somatopia.com/blog/neuroscience-somatic-techniques